BEYOND THE SWASTIKA

'The constant search, however noble or necessary, for
the wickedness of the covert neo-Nazi has blinded us
to the pernicious underside of the reformed German
liberal . . .'

Peter O'Brien's controversial study of contemporary Germany looks at mounting fears of a resurgent xenophobic
nationalism, arguing that the problem has been misinter-
preted. The real danger, he argues, is the entrenched liberalism which holds German nationalism in check.

O'Brien traces among West Germany's political elites the
appeal and uses of 'technocratic liberalism,' which, he
argues, overzealously protects Germany's liberal democracy
to the detriment of minority groups who are denied full
political participation.

This lively and original book will appeal to all those
concerned by accounts of the rising tide of nationalism in
Germany and elsewhere in Europe. It will be essential
reading for students of German history, politics, and society.

Peter O'Brien is Associate Professor of Political Science at
Trinity University, San Antonio, Texas.

BEYOND THE SWASTIKA

Peter O'Brien

London and New York

First published 1996
by Routledge
11 New Fetter Lane, London EC4P 4EE

Simultaneously published in the USA and Canada
by Routledge
29 West 35th Street, New York, NY 10001

© 1996 Peter O'Brien

Typeset in Palatino by
Ponting–Green Publishing Services, Chesham, Bucks
Printed and bound in Great Britain by
Clays Ltd, St Ives plc

British Library Cataloguing in Publication Data
A catalogue record for this book is available from
the British Library

Library of Congress Cataloguing in Publication Data
O'Brien, Peter, 1960–
Beyond the swastika / Peter O'Brien.
p.   cm.
Includes bibliographical references and index.
1. Germany–Ethnic relations. 2. Nationalism–Germany.
3. Aliens–Germany. 4. Liberalism–Germany. 5. Racism–Germany.
6. Xenophobia–Germany. I. Title.
DD76.027   1996
305.8'00943–dc20   96–19653   CIP

ISBN 0–415–13851–5 (hbk)
ISBN 0–415–13852–3 (pbk)

For Patricia M. and Gerard T. O'Brien

CONTENTS

ACKNOWLEDGEMENTS

Many persons and institutions assisted me in the completion of this book. The University of Michigan and Kalamazoo College collaborated to provide me an entire semester to start the book in Ann Arbor. Trinity University thrice sent me to Germany to collect materials relevant to the project. So many colleagues generously read and constructively criticized the manuscript that listing them all here would endanger too many trees. You all know who you are and that only I bear responsibility for the claims made. I owe a debt to Caroline Wintersgill for sticking with the project when others wanted to abandon it. A wonderful collection of family and friends helped me to keep a balanced sense of perspective and not get consumed by the writing of the manuscript. Finally, I dedicate the book to Pat and Jerry O'Brien, may he rest in peace. With their unconditional love, Mom and Dad have always given me the encouragement to pursue my goals, even if they turn out to be unpopular or controversial.

Peter O'Brien
San Antonio

1

GERMANY BETWEEN NATIONALISM AND LIBERALISM

We seek not a German Europe, rather a European Germany.
(Helmut Kohl)

INTRODUCTION

The Chancellor's paraphrase of Thomas Mann's statement tellingly reveals the nagging question surrounding united Germany. The renunciation of a 'German Europe' is plainly designed to allay ubiquitous fears of resurgent German nationalism – of a Germany now proud, strong, and bossy enough to dominate Europe again. The pledge to a 'European Germany,' by contrast, is meant as a warranty of unswerving German liberalism – of a democratic, dependable, conciliatory Germany dedicated to European integration. No one, least the Germans, doubts that united Germany will lead Europe in the future. But *Angst* abounds over whether Germany will lead the Continent backwards to the Europe of yesteryear, ravished by destructive nationalism, or forwards to a harmonious Europe of tomorrow which finally realizes the best of its lofty liberal tradition.

This grave concern over the tension between nationalist and liberal trends is hardly unique to the newly united Germany. Since the Second World War, it has been common to read all of modern German political history as a profound and protracted struggle between the opposing forces of

1

German nationalism and Western liberalism. The years before 1945 are typically depicted as a victory for the former and its nasty bedfellows. Despite the liberal heritage of the *Aufklärung* as well as sporadic flirtations with the ideas and institutions of Western liberalism, in Germany authority ultimately triumphed over liberty, obscurantism over enlightenment, utopianism over pragmatism, militarism over diplomacy, barbarity over humanity. Whether in the authoritarian Second Empire, troubled Weimar Republic, or murderous Third Reich, German nationalism always wound up smothering the faint breaths of liberalism in the land.

It was National Socialism, paradoxically, which discredited German nationalism. Defeat in and division after the war made the unity of nation and state a practical impossibility. On a deeper ethical level, the base deeds of the Nazis laid bare the moral depravity inherent in nationalist thinking. At the same time, the ignominy borne by the German people as a result of the Holocaust left them disenchanted with their own nation. In this vein Karl Jaspers wrote after the war:

> The history of the German nation-state is at an end. What we as a great nation can give ourselves and the world is insight into the situation of the world today: that nationalism today is the ruin of Europe and all other continents. While nationalism is today the paramount destructive force on earth, we can begin to grasp its roots and remove it.[1]

Thus the very liberalism the Germans so perilously eschewed before the war became their sole salvation after it. Only liberalism's respect for the dignity of the individual, it was believed, could prevent a revival of prejudice and persecution. Only its democratic political institutions could stave off the return to dictatorship. Only its penchant for rationality, compromise, and civility could insure against the

1 Karl Jaspers, *Freiheit und Wiedervereinigung* (Munich: Piper, 1960), p. 53.

hedonistic, reckless, and offensive policies which had ignited two world wars in three decades. And we have grown accustomed to understanding the history of the Federal Republic, with its anchored civil liberties, stable democracy, and amicable foreign policy, as a largely successful transformation of an entire polity and people from a nationalist to liberal orientation. Following the war, liberalism took root and blossomed in West Germany, leaving nationalism to wither in its shadow.

Still, the bitter memory of Weimar refuses to fade altogether. Then, liberal democracy succumbed to the seductive allure of nationalism. Consequently, a pall of anxiety has hung over the Federal Republic since its inception. Many Germans as well as non-Germans feel compelled to keep vigilant watch for the slightest traces of nationalist revival. In Germany, events which would appear trivial or tangential in most liberal democracies (marginal support for a xenophobic party or personality, construction of a national museum, destruction of a synagogue) can and do trigger national debates over the security and sincerity of liberal democracy in the land. German nationalism, it is feared, lies dormant, waiting to erupt and bury the liberal advancements made since the war.

It should come as no surprise, then, that concern over resurgent German nationalism has swelled in the wake of Unification. East and west Germans are again united in one state. Saddled with the burdensome economic, political, social, and cultural tasks of welding two societies, the Germans often appear self-absorbed, more disposed perhaps to neglect or ignore commitments and responsibilities to neighboring states. Furthermore, Unification, coupled with the collapse of the Soviet empire, has made Germany the strongest power in Europe, surely able, if not (yet) willing, to bully its neighbors. We witness rising sympathy in the land for the idea that the new Germany should first and foremost concern itself with the welfare of Germans and German national interests. If that were not enough cause for alarm, neo-Nazi parties and gangs have re-entered the scene. In cities like Rostock, Hoyerswerda, and Solingen, non-German minorities must daily fear for their physical safety. At times, citizens and officials seem indifferent to this cruelty in ways reminiscent if not identical to the 1930s. No level-headed observer seriously thinks Nazism or anything like it could return to menace Germany and Europe.[2] Yet, many cannot help but wonder if the scales, long tipped in favor of liberalism, may not be tipping back toward nationalism.[3] That troubling 'German Question' will not go away.

This book both explores and challenges this customary reading of postwar German politics. Borrowing a time-honored strategy from German philosophy, I set out to turn the accepted interpretation on its head. I contend that we need not so anxiously fear resurgent German nationalism because entrenched German liberalism holds it in check. On the contrary, we ought to be wary of liberalism itself. A deceptive normative bias inheres in the perceived tension between nationalism and liberalism in Germany. We automatically value all signs of liberal practices and principles, especially when they come at the expense of nationalist ones, as ethical advancements. I want to cast doubt on the presumed innocence of German liberalism.

Moreover, I want to justify this charge in that most sensitive of German political issues: minority affairs. In the postwar era, minority relations chiefly involve the issue of migration. Here it has become the norm to downplay the success of liberalism, spotlighting and condemning anti-migrant legislation as evidence of enduring German nationalism.[4] Meanwhile, the tiniest steps toward a more open and

2 Although Conor Cruise O'Brien did make such an argument in 'Beware, the Reich Is Reviving,' *The Times* (October 31, 1989).
3 See Jürgen Habermas, 'Der DM-Nationalismus,' *Die Zeit* (March 30, 1990); Michael Lerner, '"No" to German Reunification,' *Tikkun* (March/April 1990); or Arthur Miller, 'Uneasy about the Germans,' *New York Times Sunday Magazine* (May 6, 1990).
4 See, for instance, William Rogers Brubaker, *Citizenship and Nationhood in France and Germany* (Cambridge, Mass.: Harvard University Press, 1992).

liberal approach (easier visa requirements, social assistance for migrants) have been heralded as salutary, if admittedly inadequate.[5] I claim that these steps have been larger and more harmful than conventionally assumed. Put differently, this book suggests that the constant search, however noble or necessary, for the wickedness of the covert neo-Nazi has blinded us to the pernicious underside of the reformed German liberal.

LIBERALISM AND NATIONALISM DEFINED

It makes sense at this point to clarify how I define and use the concepts of liberalism and nationalism. Both have specific meanings in the German context which differ from more general definitions of the terms common elsewhere. In the broadest sense, liberalism refers to the worldview, predominant in the West, which understands itself as the legitimate offspring and heir of the European Enlightenment. Liberalism rests on three constitutive beliefs: in the freedom of all humans to determine their own destiny; in human reason as the proper arbiter of profane affairs; and in progress or self-improvement. Several institutions have since the Enlightenment become associated with liberal societies. These include among others: democratically and freely elected governments limited, however, by the guarantee of an array of civil liberties for citizens; free markets subject, however, to governmental regulation designed to prevent or lighten certain disagreeable human exigencies; legal systems, national and international, based on the rational adjudication of human disputes; and free public education open to all citizens some time during their lifetime. Finally, liberalism sustains itself through the conviction of its own earthly superiority, that is, through the belief that free, rational agents will prefer liberalism to its competitors.

5 See Lutz Hoffmann, *Die unvollendete Republik* (Frankfurt: PapyRossa Verlag, 1991).

In Germany, liberalism has a further meaning flavored by the land's history. Liberalism is understood as the political ideology which failed to predominate in Germany from the time of the Enlightenment until the end of the Second World War. Consequently, present-day liberalism in Germany also means the conspicuous absence of a host of social, political, and personal traits common to prewar Germany. These I discuss at length in Chapter 2, where I treat the development of liberalism in West Germany after the war. For now, suffice it to say that the notion of change, indeed radical change or transformation, represents a critical dimension of the meaning of liberalism in Germany. Liberalism today is very much what Germany was not yesterday.

Moreover, what Germany was is well captured by the concept 'nationalism.' Although Fritz Stern's popular epithet 'illiberalism'[6] is probably the most precise label (from a liberal perspective) for the political culture of prewar Germany, it is nevertheless true that German nationalism is generally considered to be the single greatest source of illiberalism in Germany. As a result, German nationalism has taken on a meaning which pits it against liberalism. Nationalism in Germany (and in this book) therefore has nothing to do with, say, the theory of 'liberal nationalism' espoused by many Middle Easterners who wish to encourage their country to move or remain in a liberal direction. Nor has it anything in common with pride in one's country, as the adjective 'nationalistic' conveys in, say, the USA or France.

It is precisely for this reason that Germany's foremost liberal, Jürgen Habermas, devised the clever term '*Verfassungs-patriotismus*' to connote the feeling of pride in the government of the Federal Republic of Germany. Habermas offered the term, literally 'constitution patriotism,' to those who feel pride in and loyalty to not the German nation or

6 Fritz Stern, *The Failure of Illiberalism: Essays on the Political Culture of Modern Germany* (New York: Columbia University Press, 1992).

people, but rather the government and society constituted by and since the Basic Law of 1949. In Germany, nationalism has never meant solely pride in one's government. It has meant pride in and support for the German nation (*Volk*). Moreover, it is because this nation has never been unified under one government that the term has not come to be synonymous, as in France or the USA, with a political entity. For the same reason, nationalism in Germany is at heart racism. Without a single political source of identity, 'Germans' have been defined not only as a people who share a common language and culture (the notion behind the popular German term *Kulturnation*) but also common blood or lineage (in German, *Abstammung*). In fact, the Basic Law defines *das Volk* in accordance with the legal concept of *jus sanguinis* (citizenship by blood lineage), which includes as members of the nation millions of ethnic Germans who live outside the borders of the Federal Republic.

One other crucial dimension of nationalism and liberalism in Germany deserves note. The German nation is also that group of people who collectively and historically bears responsibility for the Holocaust. Moreover, the experience of the Holocaust profoundly shapes the understanding of nationalism and liberalism. For the Germans' reckless embrace of nationalism at the expense of liberalism, it is believed, ultimately culminated in the Holocaust. Relatedly, the triumph of liberalism today is understood as the greatest safeguard against repeating the Holocaust. Resurgent nationalism causes such great alarm, then, because it is seen (and remembered) as the enemy of liberalism and the harbinger of one form of illiberalism or the other.

The pivotal position of the Holocaust in contemporary German identity makes the issue of migration particularly sensitive. Germany, of course, is no longer home to a large Jewish community. Nevertheless, like other industrial nations in Europe, it has since the 1960s attracted a sizable and seemingly permanent migrant population. By last count, resident aliens comprised 8.5 per cent of Germany's population, 6.3 per cent of France's, and 4.3 per cent of Britain's.[7] Moreover, Muslim migrants number well over 2 million in Germany, giving the land once again a significant non-Christian minority. How Germany treats its nearly 7 million non-Germans naturally is seen as a test of how well Germans have learned the lessons of the Holocaust.

As already intimated, by current popular perception the Germans are scoring poorly. Since Unification, violence against foreigners has mounted, neo-Nazi organizations have proliferated, and xenophobic parties and personalities have made electoral gains. Many view these developments as the first wave in a possible tide of nationalist revival which threatens to wash across the newly united land. Thus, election analyst Konrad Schacht warns that

the number of voters who decide in favor of the extreme right-wing parties represents only a relatively small part of the general readiness for adopting a right-wing point of view and the protest potential which exists for our society and which could be mobilized in favor of a right-wing party, e.g. in case of an economic crisis or under the strong pressure of immigration.[8]

Similarly, Eike Hennig contends that

illiberality, intolerance, crude simplification, unquestioned acceptance of fixed rules and regulations, steadfastness and the rejection of strangers ('people of a different nature') – these important hallmarks of a right-wing attitude and character – remain within the spectrum of established and accepted behavior. The majority of persons with right-wing attitudes have so

7 'Die Beauftragte der Bundesregierung für die Belange der Ausländer,' *Ausländerinnen und Ausländer in europäischen Staaten* (Bonn: Die Beauftragte der Bundesregierung für die Belange der Ausländer, 1994), pp. 54–55.

8 Quoted in Hans-Gerd Jaschke, 'Sub-Cultural Aspects of Right-Wing Extremism,' in *Political Culture in Germany,* eds Dirk Berg-Schlosser and Ralf Rytlewski (New York: St Martin's, 1993), p. 127.

far been submerged among the voters of the Christian Democratic and Christian Social Union.[9]

These findings parallel those of prominent experts on migration who argue that Germany does a poor job of assimilating immigrants. Rogers Brubaker, for instance, asserts that Germans 'lack . . . a viable assimilationist tradition.' They balk at Germanizing foreigners because of an 'ethnocultural inflection of German self-understanding' that 'requires that one become German in some thicker, richer sense than merely acquiring a new passport.'[10] Lutz Hoffmann argues that Germans cannot conceive of normality in terms of ethnic diversity, even though the latter is the norm in their land.

[I]n the feeling of solidarity [*Zusammenheitsgefühl*] found in German identity . . . foreigners have . . . no place. That is the precondition for consensus. The 'We' feeling simply does not take them into account. . . . Foreigners therefore do not count as part of the 'humans in the Federal Republic of Germany.'[11]

We are reminded of Julius Langbehn's invidious remark from the nineteenth century claiming 'a Jew could no more become a German than a plum could become an apple.'[12]

I neither agree nor disagree with these authors in terms of the way Germans view themselves and foreigners. Rather, I contest the implication in all of these works that nationalist sentiments have broad real and potential political influence in Germany. I argue that liberal persons and laws hold greater sway over Germany's policies governing minorities than do nationalist ones. Moreover, the former turn out to be aggressively assimilationist as well as discriminatory. In other words, I claim that liberalism represents a greater source of political inequality in Germany than nationalism.

9 Quoted in ibid.
10 Rogers Brubaker, *Citizenship*, pp. 177–178.
11 Hoffmann, *Die unvollendete Republik*, p. 12.
12 Quoted in Arno J. Mayer, *The Persistence of the Old Regime* (New York: Pantheon, 1981), p. 295.

How can liberalism promote inequality and discrimination in politics? It cannot, to my mind, and remain true to its tenets. Part of my argument, then, entails tracing the emergence, appeal, and influence of what I dub 'technocratic liberalism.' Here too the Holocaust plays a leading role. The Holocaust jolted liberals not merely because of its unprecedented brutality, but also because it happened in a cultured society. Liberalism thrives on converts. Its ontological and epistemological axioms promise adherents that all free and rational agents unencumbered by ignorance or fear will assent to liberalism. Before the Holocaust, most liberal leaders believed liberalism could spread by virtue of its natural appeal alone. Listen to Woodrow Wilson's boundless optimism in 1893 regarding the prospects for democracy:

> If Aristocracy seems about to disappear, Democracy seems about universally to prevail. Ever since the rise of popular education in the last century and its vast development since have assured a thinking weight to the masses of people everywhere, the advance of democratic opinion and the spread of democratic institutions have been most marked and significant. They have destroyed almost all pure forms of Monarchy and Aristocracy by introducing into them imperative forces of popular thought and the concrete institutions of popular representation; and they promise to reduce politics to a single pure form by excluding all other governing forces and institutions but those of a wide suffrage and a democratic representation – by reducing all forms of government to democracy.[13]

The Germans spoiled liberal optimism, particularly in the Weimar Republic. Germany had a modern economy, educated populace, and, after 1918, a liberal democratic constitution. And yet Germany soon thereafter spurned liberalism

13 Woodrow Wilson, *The State* (Boston: D.C. Heath, 1893).

and imperiled, in the Second World War, its very survival. The logic of liberalism had not really to that point made allowance for this possibility.

After the war, leading Western liberals took pains to prevent the recurrence of the German disaster. As will become clear in Chapter 2, they set out to insure liberalism rather than rely on its natural appeal. They channeled their efforts into three chief goals:

1 to provide an environment (especially socio-economic) conducive to liberalism rather than illiberalism;
2 to educate would-be liberals in the principles of liberalism rather than rely on persons' reason alone naturally to guide them aright; and
3 to test to make sure persons become and remain genuine liberals rather than assume so, based on the superiority of liberalism.

These three endeavors taken together form what I call 'technocratic liberalism.' Chapter 2 deals with its emergence in West Germany after the war, while Chapters 3, 4, and 5 analyze its effects on policies pertaining to minorities in the postwar era.

CAVEATS

Beyond the fine distinction between liberalism and technocratic liberalism, other caveats merit mention. In many spots, the text will sound highly critical of liberalism (actually technocratic liberalism). Some readers may find the work irksomely slanted, because I ignore the many desirable achievements wrought in Germany through the triumph of liberalism. I am hardly unaware or unappreciative of these. The Holocaust or anything like it has not recurred. German foreign policy has been mostly conciliatory. Germany guarantees extensive social and civil rights and privileges – something which helps make it Europe's most attractive destination for migrants and refugees. But I aim to refute the bias, particularly pronounced in relations with minorities, that liberalism has only positive political consequences. I seek to uncover negative consequences which go unnoticed due to the Manichaeanistic relationship assumed between nationalism and liberalism. I offer here, then, not a balanced assessment of the costs and benefits of liberalism, rather a sharp focus on its costs.

I should also warn that this book is not yet another case for German exceptionalism. Indeed, the idea that Germany is different represents a major assumption of the nationalism-vs.-liberalism paradigm I challenge. Although I do think the legacy of the Holocaust makes Germany unique in some ways which should become clear as the argument unfolds, the Federal Republic generally faces very similar issues regarding minorities that most advanced industrial democracies face. I focus solely on Germany for reasons of limiting scope, and because I know its politics best. I do not wish to imply that technocratic liberalism is unique to Germany. I can well imagine that technocratic liberalism has the same kinds of political effects in other countries as those I highlight for Germany. Indeed, Étienne Balibar discerns a global and epochal transformation taking place from discrimination based on the ascriptive traits of nation and race to that based on the kind of acquired traits liberalism generates in its adherents:

> It may well be that the current variants of neoracism are merely a transitional ideological formation, which is destined to develop towards discourses and social technologies in which the aspect of the historical recounting of genealogical myths (the play of substitutions between race, people, culture and nation) will give way . . . to the aspect of psychological assessment of intellectual aptitudes and dispositions to 'normal' social life (or, conversely, to criminality and deviance), and to 'optimal' reproduction . . . aptitudes and dispositions which a battery of cognitive, sociopsychological and statistical sciences would then undertake

12

to measure, select and monitor, striking a balance between hereditary and environmental factors. . . . In other words, that ideological formation would develop towards a 'post racism.'[14]

Of course, Max Weber long ago perceived the growing significance of acquired at the expense of ascribed traits as a hallmark of modernity. It is thus doubtful that technocratic liberalism is unique to Germany.[15]

I should add that this book really is not about 'the Germans' as a people. Many prominent analyses of Germany sport titles which purport to capture the essence of Germanness, of what it means to Germans to be German: *German Identity, The German Mind*, or simply *The Germans*. Books of this sort tend to anthropomorphize the concept of nation. The authors often ascribe human attributes – attitudes, motives, even behaviors – to the German population *as a whole*. In a curious vestige of Nazi ideology, *das Volk* assumes a life, mind, and spirit of its own which transcends and ultimately defines the individual Germans who comprise it. Such works leave readers, often unintentionally, with the impression that all Germans think and act alike. Thus, 'the Germans today are one of the least chauvinistic of major Western countries';[16] they have 'an almost neurotic sensitivity to signs of economic trouble accompanied by a tendency . . . to react with pessimism and undemocratic behavior';[17] or they 'are less disposed than others to ignore the remonstrances and reservations of neighbors.'[18]

14 'Is There a "NeoRacism"?,' in *Race, Nation, Class*, eds Étienne Balibar and Immanuel Wallerstein (London: Verso, 1991), p. 26.
15 Also see Thomas Spragens, *The Irony of Liberal Reason* (Chicago: The University of Chicago Press, 1981) for a thorough discussion of liberalism's susceptibility to technocracy.
16 John Ardagh, *Germany and the Germans* (New York: Harper & Row, 1987), p. 254.
17 Gordon Craig, *The Germans* (New York: Meridian, 1982), p. 294.
18 Werner Weidenfeld, 'Die Identität der Deutschen – Fragen, Positionen, Perspektiviven,' in *Die Identität der Deutschen*, ed. Werner Weidenfeld (Bonn: Bundeszentrale für politische Bildung, 1983), p. 17.

I make no pretense to understanding or characterizing 'the Germans.' My analysis pertains only to the German intelligentsia. In the broadest sense, the German intelligentsia comprises all university-educated persons who feel an interest in and a responsibility for Germany's destiny and find themselves in positions of influence. This 'cartel of elites,' to invoke Ralf Dahrendorf's appellative,[19] ranges across the public and private sectors into the higher echelons of government, business, academy, and church. The most prominent members of the intelligentsia tend to come out of the woodwork during times of perceived national emergency and publicize their views in a deliberate attempt to sway public opinion and influence public policy.[20] By no means do these intellectuals see eye to eye on everything. Competition and conflict exist among them. However, as Peter Katzenstein notes, this 'interlocking grid' of persons, as well as of formal and informal structures of communication linking them in a 'tight policy network,' can and often does perform in a highly cooperative, concentrated, and effective manner.[21] The intricate details concerning who these elites are and how they operate will have to wait until later chapters.

For now, it is important to note that I follow Katzenstein's lead in one other significant way. Like him, I see German public policy as remarkably resilient to drastic and abrupt change. Gone are the days when an adept demagogue from outside the elite network could organize a movement and oust Germany's leaders; gone are the days when an economic downturn could cause public policy paralysis or failure. Similarly, I argue below that technocratic liberalism

19 Ralf Dahrendorf, *Society and Democracy in Germany* (New York: W.W. Norton, 1967), p. 255.
20 See, for instance, the authors who voiced opinion over Unification, reprinted in Harold James and Marla Stone, eds, *When the Wall Came Down* (London: Routledge, 1992); or those who engaged in the 'historians' debate' of 1986 in *Historikerstreit* (Munich: Piper, 1987).
21 Peter Katzenstein, *Policy and Politics in West Germany* (Philadelphia: Temple University Press, 1987), p. 35.

has incrementally grown to become a more powerful force in public policy toward minorities than nationalism and stands in no immediate danger of being swamped by it either. Many readers may find this position imprudent, even impudent, when it comes to relations with minorities. And this field is replete with pundits who warn of impending disaster. But, as the argument below will tell, this exaggerated (but understandable) fear of a reversion to Nazism or something like it helps to generate the very technocratic liberalism which politically harms Germany's minorities.

METHODOLOGY

Finally, a word about methodology is in order. Three methodologies run parallel to one another throughout the work. The first stems from my focus on the intelligentsia and comes out of the tradition of the history of ideas. In an oft-cited essay on '"Objectivity" in Social Science and Social Policy,' Max Weber discussed how human beings, in an effort to understand and act in their world, perforce devise and depend on simplifying concepts to order and make sense of an otherwise infinitely complex and chaotic reality. We slice reality into neat categories so as to be able to piece together a meaningful, though inescapably and at times imperceptibly partial, view of our complicated world. Weber went on to contend that these conceptual artifices or *Weltanschauungen* inevitably rest on, and therefore exude, normative judgements. They are 'value-laden.' We use them not only to determine how our world is, but how it ought to be.[22] Other prominent writers in the history of ideas have employed different labels: Heidegger's *Entbergung*, Gadamer's *Horizont*, Kuhn's 'paradigm,' Foucault's *episteme*. Despite great differences in the exact meanings of these concepts for their authors, each concept points to that admittedly

22 Max Weber, '"Objectivity" in Social Science and Social Policy,' in *The Methodology of the Social Sciences*, eds Edward Shils and Henry Finch (Glencoe, Ill.: The Free Press, 1949), pp. 72–111.

amorphous phenomenon of ideas (sometimes conscious, sometimes unconscious) significantly shaping our actions.

Below I make the case that technocratic liberalism, born of the perceived conflict between liberalism and nationalism, represents such a phenomenon in minority relations in Germany. In making the argument, I use approaches typical in the field of the history of ideas. Thus, I often do hermeneutic textual analysis (on statements and studies on minorities) in an effort to 'read between the lines' of what intellectuals write. I also devote considerable time to analyzing how German intellectuals define or construct an image of minorities. Here I draw from prominent thinkers who study 'the Other' (Said), 'deviance' (Foucault), '*différance*' (Derrida). Again, I acknowledge the profound differences between these authors. I am interested in the insight, common to all of them, that the way we define persons we consider alien to us reveals much about ourselves.

This highly interpretive methodology is far from flawless. It tends to downplay the influence of more concrete, material forces, like sheer greed or practical necessity, in human events. It also does not account well or at all for the unpredictable and the unintended. Aware of these short-comings, I do not present this work as a comprehensive explanation of Germany's policies toward minorities. Avarice, ambition, ignorance, necessity, fortune, and many other factors play a role in determining policies. I wish, however, to show that a worldview of technocratic liberalism also plays a role, because I seek to expose its deleterious political consequences.

Second, I also employ methods from the empiricist tradition in the social sciences. These apply particularly to my claim that policies of a liberal bent outweigh ones with a nationalist orientation. This claim I back up with tangible, traceable evidence customary in the social sciences. However, in the interest of not burdening the prose with heaps of facts and figures which interest only a few specialists, I make liberal use of footnotes that refer to sources where evidence exists in greater detail. Some readers who wish to have 'all the evidence' presented before them may find this stylistic choice irritating. I remind them of Bernard Crick's complaint: 'I am constantly depressed by the capacity of academics to overcomplicate things.'[23] I have done my best, in other words, to keep the book brief and to the point.

Third, the book follows the form of a narrative. That is, I tell the chronologically organized story of how technocratic liberalism evolved first in relation to West Germans (Chapter 2), then in relation to resident aliens (Chapters 3 and 4) and finally in relation to east Germans (Chapter 5). Haskell Fain has defended storytelling as a form of explanation different from, but not necessarily inferior to, causal explanation used in the sciences.[24] I do not wish to delve here into the complicated debate in the philosophy of history which surrounds this assertion. I need only say that I narrate the remaining chapters in the hope that, by the end of the story, readers will have a richer and fuller understanding of how technocratic liberalism evolved and operates in the Federal Republic than I could convey in formal hypotheses and conclusions. So let us get on with the story; it begins with the physical and moral ruin that was Germany by May 8, 1945.

23 Bernard Crick, *In Defence of Politics* (Chicago: University of Chicago Press, 1992), p. 7.
24 Haskell Fain, *Between Philosophy and History* (Princeton: Princeton University Press, 1970).

2

ESCAPING THE PAST

The smell of death overwhelmed us even before we passed through the stockade. More than 3,200 naked, emaciated bodies had been flung into shallow graves. Others lay in the streets where they had fallen. Lice crawled over the yellowed skin of their sharp, bony frames.

(Omar Bradley)

INTRODUCTION

Germans live in the shadow of their awful past. Much of the Federal Republic's history has centered around trying to understand the mistakes which led to Nazism in the past and trying to avoid them in the present. This effort has involved nothing less than the attempt completely to remake a people and polity. It formally began under Allied supervision in 1945 at '*Stunde Null*' ('hour zero') when Germany and the Germans were to be severed from their aberrant past and linked to a common future with their victors. The (West) Germans were to receive not just a new state, but a new collective identity as well. And the state was to be democratic rather than authoritarian, the identity liberal rather than German.

Put differently, the Allied occupiers, first, and German political leaders, later, stood before no less formidable a task than constructing a new nation-state in Europe. The concepts

18

of an abnormal German nationalism and a normal Western liberalism came to guide the thoughts and actions of the elites who shaped West Germany's destiny. Nationalism symbolized all that had gone wrong with Germany in the past, culminating in Hitler and the Holocaust. Liberalism stood for all that needed to be done to and for West Germany in the future to prevent yet another revival of German nationalism with its deadly likelihood of a third world war. All traces of excessive nationalism were to be excised from state, society, and citizenry while liberal institutions and values were to be established, encouraged, and enforced. Needless to say, the geopolitical concern of halting the advance of communism figured prominently in the decision to tie the Federal Republic to the Western Alliance. And in the opinion of the Allies, a full-scale transformation to liberalism seemed the most durable, if not most immediate, bond with the West.

Two different interpretations of and approaches to German nationalism and Western liberalism formed during and after the war. A more philosophical outlook saw German nationalism as a kind of collective character flaw which could only be remedied through vigorous re-education in liberal values. A more social scientific view analyzed German nationalism as a predictable pathological response to a certain social structural environment and prescribed broad institutional and societal change to create an environment conducive to liberalism. Eventually, Allied and West German elites employed the prescriptions of both to devise and deploy a blueprint for the re-education and reconstruction of West Germany.

RE-EDUCATION

Plans for the re-education of the German people originated in the US State Department in 1942. As war's end drew nearer, re-education initially received scant attention due to the stronger appeal to President Roosevelt of the

Morgenthau Plan to destroy and 'pastoralize' Germany. However, over the course of 1944, the Secretaries of War and State lobbied hard for a rehabilitative rather than punitive approach to Germany; and the Morgenthau Plan's appeal waned. Even before the war in Europe ceased, pilot projects in re-education were tried out on German POWs in the USA.[1]

As the Western Allies conquered across Germany, they began putting their plans into action. Radio and newspapers attracted the Allies as effective tools for re-education. In the American zone, the Office of Military Government's Information Control Division (which had been the psychological warfare branch during wartime) assumed responsibility for the media. It and its British counterpart swiftly shut down the 1,500 existing Nazi newspapers and replaced them with Allied Army publications in German. By late June 1945, the Allies began licensing independent German newspapers and radio stations so long as they had politically pluralistic editorial boards. These and many other steps created a national media for West Germany which would, for the most part, go on to endorse Anglo-American norms and values.[2]

Naturally, the schools represented another target of the re-education campaign. The Potsdam Protocol stipulated that 'German education shall be so controlled as completely to eliminate Nazi and militarist doctrines and to make possible the successful development of democratic ideas.'[3] Upon occupation, the schools were closed and their faculties and curricula subjected to the scrutiny of Allied officers with orders to purge Nazi personnel and pedagogy. In the American zone during 1945, the Education and Religious Affairs Branch dismissed teachers at a rate of 1:2. Simultaneously, the Branch sponsored emergency teacher-training

---

1 See Ron Robin, *The Barbed-Wire College* (Princeton: Princeton University Press, 1995).

2 See Dennis L. Bark and David R. Gress, *A History of West Germany,* vol. I (Oxford: Basil Blackwell, 1989), pp. 155–164.

3 Quoted in ibid., pp. 165–166.

courses in Western liberal pedagogy across the zone.[4] By the fall of 1945, 5 million textbooks had arrived in the West to replace Nazi textbooks; and the schools reopened. It is true that the Western Allies never fully completed denazification, most notably in the universities. Furthermore, despite US efforts, the hierarchical three-tiered structure of the primary and secondary educational system remained intact. As in most other facets of the occupation, the Western Allies left much for their West German successors to complete. Nevertheless, the re-education measures of the Allies marked a significant step toward a public West German educational system dedicated to the rearing of a liberal citizenry.

Behind re-education efforts lay a steadfast belief in the superiority and eventual universality of liberal values as well as in the transformative power of education to convert non-liberals to liberalism. Germany had spawned too few liberal sages, and their teachings had not been observed. Germans had remained obscured from the radiant glow of the Enlightenment. Still, its brilliant light could one day shine in Germany if its people were properly exposed to it.

Not surprisingly, unflattering portraits of the Germans abounded in the Allied countries during the war. Richard Brickner's popular *Is Germany Incurable?* limned the Germans as collectively paranoid and megalomaniacal and vilified virtually every aspect of their society, culture, and history.[5] Such blanket depictions of the inveterate flaws in the German national character continued after the war:

> At various periods of their history, and particularly in the nineteenth century, the Germans have believed with a desperate conviction . . . that they have a divine mission, that Germany has been singled out by Providence. By virtue of a superior right and sustained by

4 James F. Tent, *Mission on the Rhine* (Chicago: University of Chicago Press, 1982), p. 69.
5 Richard Brickner, *Is Germany Incurable?* (Philadelphia: J.B. Lippincott Co., 1943). For a similar view from Britain, see Rohan D'O. Butler, *The Roots of National Socialism 1783–1933* (London: Faber & Faber, 1941).

Prussian arms, the Germanic Community, they have thought, must prevail over its own members, over their many activities, and over the means by which its pre-eminence can be assured. This irrational and fervent faith is the outcome of a historical development which, throughout the centuries, gives the German imagination, with its combination of fanatical nationalism and preoccupation with internal cohesion, precedents which it can never forget and on which it builds up limitless aspirations.[6]

In the eyes of these analysts, irrationality, obscurantism, authority, and evil had triumphed over reason, Enlightenment, freedom, and goodness.

Discoveries at the death camps and testimonies at the Nuremberg Trials peaked interest in Hitler – in his barbarity and popularity. For example, in Alan Bullock's widely read biography of Hitler, the author painstakingly revealed 'the true nature of the man ... in all its naked ugliness.'[7] If Hitler's wickedness was undeniable, so was his popularity. Near the end of the war, surveys of the Psychological Warfare Division of Supreme Headquarters showed that Hitler's confidence rating among German soldiers remained at 60 per cent despite massive retreat.[8] Only 25 per cent of the German population were thought to be opponents of the Nazi regime.[9] Moreover, as late as 1951, an alarming 42 per cent of the population still felt that Germany was 'best off' during the years 1933 to 1939.[10]

6 Edmond Vermeil, 'The Origin, Nature and Development of German Nationalist Ideology in the 19th and 20th Centuries,' in *The Third Reich*, ed. Vermeil (London: Weidenfeld & Nicolson, 1955), p. 6. For a similar view, see William Shirer, *The Rise and Fall of the Third Reich* (New York: Simon & Schuster, 1960), pp. 90–113.

7 Alan Bullock, *Hitler: A Study in Tyranny* (London: Odhams Press, 1952), p. 8.

8 Robin, *Barbed-Wire College*, p. 21.

9 Michael Balfour, *West Germany: A Contemporary History* (New York: St Martin's, 1982), p. 126.

10 Institut für Demoskopie, *Jahrbuch der öffentlichen Meinung*, vol. V (Allensbach am Bodensee: Verlag für Demoskopie, 1974), p. 223.

Hitler's mass appeal triggered interest in patterns of social-ization. The German family came under close scrutiny. Most students of German society were familiar with the work carried out by the Institute for Social Research in Frankfurt in the 1930s on the authoritarian German family.[11] In 1948, Bertram Schaffner, psychiatrist at the Information Control Division Screening Center in the American zone during 1946, published his analysis of the German family based on examinations carried out at the Center. He reported:

> Family life revolves around the figure of the father. He is omnipotent, omniscient, and omnipresent, as far as this is possible for a human being. He is the source of all the authority, all the security, all the wisdom that his children expect to receive. Every other member of the family has lower status and lesser rights than his.

And according to Schaffner, this authoritarianism translated into national politics:

> What makes the study of the German family so crucial is the remarkable parallel between the rules that govern it and the credos of national, political life. . . . The study of the development of the child therefore helps us to understand the mechanisms at work in the adult in the larger 'family life' of the nation.[12]

But criticism (and self-criticism) fell hardest on the German intelligentsia. A.J.P. Taylor's question – 'why so few of the educated, civilized classes recognized Hitler as the em-bodiment of evil'[13] – haunted intellectuals, German and non-German alike. Before the war, indeed before the Nazi seizure of power, Thomas Mann criticized the tradition of

11 These studies culminated in the influential work sponsored by the American Jewish Committee: T.W. Adorno, Else Frenkel-Brunswik, Daniel J. Levinson, and R. Nevitt Sanford, *The Authoritarian Personality* (New York: Harper & Brothers, 1950).

12 Bertram Schaffner, *Fatherland: A Study of Authoritarianism in the German Family* (New York: Columbia University Press, 1948), pp. 15 and 4.

13 A.J.P. Taylor, 'The Seizure of Power,' in Vermeil, *Third Reich*, p. 525.

apolitical idealism in which he and his fellow intellectuals were steeped:

> It may seem bold to make a connection between the radical nationalism of today and the ideas of a romanticizing philosophy; nevertheless the connection exists and must be recognized by anyone who wants to understand the context of the present developments. ... We find here a certain ideology of philologists, a romanticism of professional Germanists, a superstitious faith in the Nordic – all these emanate from the academic-professorial classes.[14]

During the war, Karl Popper set to work on his influential volumes, *The Poverty of Historicism* and *The Open Society and Its Enemies*, which attacked utopian philosophy as the great enemy of liberal democracy. Although Popper arraigned all utopian thought, German philosophers bore much of his criticism.[15]

After the war, investigations of the intelligentsia's complicity in the Holocaust proliferated. In his lectures at the newly opened Heidelberg University during 1945–1946, eminent Karl Jaspers told packed halls that all Germans, including the educated, should feel a sense of collective moral responsibility for the crimes committed by the Third Reich.[16] In 1957, Leonard Krieger argued that the liberal tradition in Germany, stretching back through Hegel to Kant, had been repeatedly subsumed and spoiled by idealist collectivism. Krieger in no way directly blamed Hegel, Kant, or other German thinkers for the Nazi dictatorship. But he clearly wished to show how and why German liberals were philosophically predisposed to support, or at least tolerate, a dictator promising to realize a utopian community.

14 Quoted in Fritz Stern, *The Politics of Cultural Despair* (Berkeley: University of California Press, 1961), p. 292.
15 See, in particular, *The Open Society and Its Enemies*, vol. II (London: Routledge, 1945).
16 These were published as *Die Schuldfrage* (Heidelberg: L. Schneider, 1946).

A few years later, Fritz Stern vitiated the entire German *Bürgertum*. Throughout the Second Empire, their 'vulgar idealism' 'became more and more of a political force, it became in fact the rhetoric with which the unpolitical German denounced the mass society, democracy, liberalism, modernity, indeed all the so-called importations from the West.' Stern, in contrast to Krieger, did not demur in assigning direct blame:

In a very real sense, the Hitler movement was idealistic, and that was the condition of its success. Did it not inveigh against materialism and selfishness, defy reality, promise the end of fratricidal conflict and the establishment of social harmony, of unity and leadership, power and confidence? To make it appear that his party's nihilism was really idealism, its resentful and cowardly brutality virile strength – that was Hitler's greatest propagandistic success. The unpolitical, the educated German hesitated. It was not the few men of culture that joined the party before 1933 that promoted Hitler's success, but the many that failed to oppose him, failed not out of fear, but out of uncertainty lest this be the untamed Caesar, the real Germanic savior.[17]

Within Germany, Kurt Sontheimer laid the blame for the collapse of the Weimar Republic on the doorstep of German intellectuals. Their relentless attacks on liberal democracy, he averred, 'spiritually tore the rug out from under the democratic Republic and obliterated its public confidence. . . . [O]nly in a democratic state without a secure public confidence was the mass success of an NSDAP possible.'[18]

Later in the 1960s, Fritz Ringer, Peter Gay, and George

17 'The Political Consequences of the Unpolitical German,' reprinted in Fritz Stern, *The Failure of Illiberalism* (New York: Columbia University Press, 1992), pp. 18, 23.
18 Kurt Sontheimer, *Antidemokratisches Denken in der Weimarer Republik* (Munich: Nymphenburger Verlagshandlung, 1962), p. 19.

Mosse separately published scathing reproaches of the German intelligentsia. Ringer took aim at the professoriate. Germany's mandarins, as he called them to emphasize their powerful influence throughout society, 'helped to destroy the Republic, without having chosen its successor. . . . They nourished a whole series of semiconscious illusions which prevented the rational discussion of political alternatives and discredited every possible mode of social and cultural adjustment to modernity.'[19] Gay went beyond the universities and pointed the finger at the entire cultural elite. Hardly a single intellectual luminary escaped his blacklist of those who, in one way or the other, nourished the Nazi movement by eschewing Western liberalism and espousing utopianism. 'In calling for something higher than politics,' he judged, they 'helped to pave the way for something lower – barbarism.'[20] Mosse hammered the final nail in the coffin with his devastating argument that anti-Semitism – the vilest ideology of Germany's history – was a natural outgrowth of the German intellectual tradition. 'The Jew came to stand for all that these men feared: materialism, progress, the big city, and the sober rationalistic mind that could have no sense of the beautiful.'[21]

Their tradition sullied, West German savants had little recourse after the war but to recant and convert. And although material incentives doubtless enticed them, German elites underwent something akin to a spiritual conversion or awakening. They trumpeted Western beliefs and behaviors and prescribed them to their people. Mann set an early, conspicuous example when after the war he refused to return to the fatherland to live. Ralf Dahrendorf later moved across the Channel to Britain. Friedrich Meinecke

---

19 Fritz Ringer, *The Decline of the German Mandarins* (Cambridge, Mass.: Harvard University Press, 1969), p. 446.

20 Peter Gay, *Weimar Culture* (New York: Harper & Row, 1968), p. 69.

21 George Mosse, *Germans and Jews* (New York: Howard Fertig, 1970), p. 37; also see his *The Crisis of German Ideology* (London: Weidenfeld & Nicolson, 1966).

urged Germans to assist the Allies in their mission 'to eradicate National Socialism and thereby provide the atmosphere for Christian Occidental sound morals.'[22] Sontheimer declared that the Nazi debacle had proven once and for all that liberal democracy was the only humane political system.[23] Karl Dietrich Bracher felt obligated to compile for his fellow citizens 'a catalog of Western values' (individualism, pluralism, pragmatism, self-criticism) which he found best exemplified in the United States.[24] Friedrich Sell chided his compatriots for being too serious, and thus too intolerant, and urged them to assume the 'live and let live' attitude of Americans.[25] It was as if Goethe and Schiller's exhortation from *Xenien* had finally pierced through the cacophony of German nationalism: 'You hope in vain, Germans, to form yourself into a nation; develop yourselves instead, as certainly as you can, into human beings.'

These and other esteemed scholars lent vital support to the fledgling democracy and reinforced its legitimacy. In this way, the intelligentsia acquired a philosophical and personal stake in the success of the FRG and the collective transformation of the West German citizenry. As will become clear below, the intelligentsia came to fancy itself the republic's watchdog for liberalism and democracy against abiding or resurgent nationalism and authoritarianism. For despite their enthusiasm for liberalism, these liberal watchdogs harbored a deep-seated suspicion of the abiding allure of German nationalism and all its trappings. The fear of an impending relapse into the loathsome habits of the past would profoundly influence the project of building the new republic as much as the determination to emulate the West; so much so, that it would come to form the *raison d'être* of

22 Friedrich Meinecke, *The German Catastrophe*, trans. Sidney Fay (Boston: Beacon, 1950), p. 104.
23 Sontheimer, *Antidemokratisches Denken*, p. 399.
24 Karl Dietrich Bracher, *Deutschland zwischen Demokratie und Diktatur* (Munich: Scherz, 1964), pp. 313ff.
25 Friedrich Sell, *Die Tragödie des deutschen Liberalismus* (Stuttgart: Verlags-Anstalt, 1953), p. 448.

statemakers. Eventually, the West German intelligentsia would take immense pride not only in the fact that they liberalized themselves and their people, but in particular, that they did so despite themselves. The achievement of Westernization would turn out to be so sweet because it was considered so unlikely, so unGerman.

RECONSTRUCTION

Not all scholars agreed that liberal re-education would suffice to extirpate belligerent German nationalism. In 1942, Talcott Parsons warned that the

typical German character structure . . . is supported by, and closely interdependent with, an institutional structure of German society. The interdependence is such that on the one hand any permanent and far-reaching change in the orientation of the German people probably cannot rest on a change of character structure alone, but must also involve institutional change; otherwise, institutional conditions would continue to breed the same type of character structure in new generations.[26]

Parsons, of course, ranks as one of the founders of the school of structural functionalism, which came to predominate in the social sciences during the 1950s and 1960s. Structural functionalists downplay human free agency and underscore the power of structural forces outside individuals' control to determine behavior. From this perspective, it was not so much the Germans as their environment that was to blame for the Nazi debacle. Structural functionalists stressed the differences between the process of modernization in the West and in Germany – differences which stimulated a different perception of and experience with modernity.

26 'The Problem of Controlled Institutional Change,' reprinted in Talcott Parsons, *Essays in Sociological Theory* (Glencoe, Ill.: Free Press, 1949), p. 238.

Recognition of Germany's peculiar modernization antedated the formal conceptualization of structural functionalism. As early as 1911, Winston Churchill is known to have characterized Germany as a modern power controlled, however, by a feudal elite.[27] In 1915, Thorsten Veblen claimed that Germany had undergone an industrial revolution but without abolishing the feudal social structure or authoritarian state.[28] During the war, Harold Laski reiterated this view:

Germany did not, like France and England, ever have a middle-class revolution. Like Japan her industrialization was the outcome of an alliance between business men, on the one hand, and the army, the aristocracy and the bureaucrats on the other – an alliance, moreover, in which the business men always remained the junior partners. For throughout the imperial period, the pivotal positions in the state always remained in the hands of the same class that held them in the eighteenth century. Germany, until the close of the war of 1914, was, in fact, an eighteenth-century state disposing of the power of modern technology; the greatest event in its history during the nineteenth and twentieth centuries was the revolution which did not happen.

When in the Weimar Republic Germany began to develop many of the elements of Western modernity, Germans, accustomed to a different modernity, reacted in predictable pathological ways. Each of Hitler's supporters sought through his leadership to escape or avoid the feared Western modernity and return to or recapture the familiar German modernity of the past:

[T]he business men who thought that the conditions of profitability would be resumed when the trade unions

27 See Richard J. Evans, 'The Myth of Germany's Missing Revolution,' *New Left Review* (January/February 1985): 68.
28 Thorsten Veblen, *Imperial Germany and the Industrial Revolution* (London: Macmillan, 1915).

had been destroyed, the petit bourgeois shopkeeper who thought that he would be freed from the dangerous competition of the chain-store, the working-man who was heartened by the promise that the tyranny of interest would be destroyed, the soldier who yearned for the opportunity to wipe out the shame, as he thought it, of Versailles. All of them, not with unity of purpose, but for contradictory purposes, united to serve the outlaw's ambitions. All of them were hypnotized into identifying his ambition with their own. All of them were deluded by the faith partly that, when he attained power, he would be their man.[29]

This view of the causes of dictatorship steadily increased its proponents with the increase in the influence of structural functionalism, reaching its apex in 1966 with the publication of Barrington Moore's *Social Origins of Dictatorship and Democracy*.

Inside Germany, the structural functionalist approach received a big boost in the 1950s from historian Karl Dietrich Bracher. He showed how a broad array of social and political forces led to the *Dissolution of the Weimar Republic*.[30] It was Ralf Dahrendorf, however, who most popularized this interpretation. In 1967, he published the paradigmatic portrait of Germany's peculiar path (*Sonderweg*) through modernity. In his endeavor to answer 'What it is in German society that may account for Germany's failure to give home to democracy in its liberal sense,'[31] he looked to the 'structures of

29 Harold Laski, *Reflections on the Revolution of Our Time* (London: George Allen & Unwin, 1943), pp. 99, 109. Other interpretations of the Germans as pathological reactors to a specific environment which appeared before the end of the war are: Arthur Rosenberg, *A History of the German Republic*, trans. I.F.D. Morrow and L.M. Sieveking (New York: Russell & Russell, 1965); and Erich Fromm, *Escape from Freedom* (New York: Rinehart, 1941).

30 Karl Dietrich Bracher, *Auflösung der Weimarer Republik* (Stuttgart: Ring-Verlag, 1955).

31 Ralf Dahrendorf, *Society and Democracy in Germany* (New York: W.W. Norton, 1967), p.14.

German society'[32] formed in the nineteenth century. German industrialization, in contrast to French, American, and English, was 'late and rapid, but also thorough.'[33] This meant that the state, dominated by the aristocracy, had to play a larger role in directing industrialization. Hence,

[i]ndustrialization in Germany failed to produce a self-confident bourgeoisie with its own political aspirations. In so far as a bourgeoisie emerged at all, it remained relatively small and, what is more, unsure of itself and dependent in its social and political standards. As a result, German society lacked the stratum that in England and America, and to a lesser extent even in France, had been the moving force of a development in the direction of greater modernity and liberalism.[34]

'Instead of developing it, industrialization in Germany swallowed the liberal principle.'[35] Germany evolved into 'an industrial feudal society with an authoritarian welfare state' rather than a modern industrial society with a liberal democracy.[36] When liberal democracy finally came to Germany after the First World War, it came in form but not in spirit. As Hitler's rise to power attested, Weimar did not have enough citizens who truly believed in liberal principles to fend off attacks on democracy. 'Germany could – and possibly had to – step on the path to National Socialist dictatorship because her society bore many traits that resisted the constitution of liberty.'[37]

This view of Germany as a modernized society without a modernized (that is, liberal) citizenry took on the character of a Kuhnian paradigm in the 1960s and 1970s. It eclipsed all

32 Ibid., p. 336.
33 Ibid., p. 34.
34 Ibid., p. 49.
35 Ibid., p. 39.
36 Ibid., p. 60.
37 Ibid., p. 36.

other schools of thought and became the definitive story of Germany's past.[38]

It takes no genius to spot in the structural functionalist diagnosis of Germany's ills the implied cure: a strong dose of liberal Western social structures. It is true that initially the Allies intended to put the occupation to mainly destructive ends. Three of the famous 'Four Ds' – denazification, decartelization, dismantling, and democratization – clearly aimed to smash the social structure that fostered Nazism. Denazification – which ranged from the high-profile Nuremberg Trials to the low-profile inquisitive questionnaires sent to 1.4 million Germans – resulted (in the Western zones) in criminal sentences of varying severity for little more than 10,000 persons and termination of employment for some 58,000 civil servants (*Beamte*). But the processes were terminated on March 31, 1948 (in the US zone).[39] Of course, on May 8, 1945, the entire German military ceased operations as part of the surrender and was fully replaced by Allied soldiers. Yet, the West German military was reactivated in 1951. In the Western zones, 415 factories were slotted for dismantling in 1946 but most remained intact due to a reversal in policy later that same year.[40]

As is well known, Western distrust of the Soviets billowed in 1946 and eventually led to the constructive decision to rebuild western Germany into a sturdy ally against communism. Beginning with the creation of Bizonia and its Economic Council in 1946–1947 and running through the Marshall Plan, the currency reform, the formation of the OEEC and GATT in 1948, and finally the establishment of the European Coal and Steel Community in 1951 and the Common Market

38 See the review of this school of historiography in David Blackbourn and Geoff Eley, *The Peculiarities of German History* (Oxford: Oxford University Press, 1984).

39 For details, see Bark and Gress, *A History of West Germany,* vol. I, pp. 74–89. The West German government did continue to try hundreds of cases after 1949. See the same pages for details.

40 Ibid., p. 176.

in 1957, the Allies, with West German cooperation, erected the building blocks of a market economy which could support a dominant bourgeoisie. Militarily, commencing with the formation of NATO in 1948 through the European Common Defense in 1951 and ending in the Federal Republic's inclusion in NATO in 1954, West Germany obtained a secure military apparatus absent of the politically and socially powerful officer corps common in the past. Politically, with the selective licensing of democratic parties in 1945, the first *Land* elections in 1946, the convening of the Constituent Assembly in 1948, and Allied approval of the Basic Law in 1949, West Germany acquired a liberal democratic political architecture with strong safeguards against authoritarianism.

In spite of these dramatic steps, doubt over whether the elaborate cure would work on the Germans loomed large. Distrust of the Germans would not vanish. Thus NATO and the EEC not only assisted West Germany, they also gave the Allies continued partial control over critical dimensions of its society. Admittedly, in 1955 the Allied High Commission returned sovereignty to the West Germans, but the Allies retained troops in the Federal Republic along with reserved emergency powers to protect them. And as far as the Constituent Assembly was concerned, the delegates were hardly at liberty to draft a document solely of their own choosing. The Anglo-American–French Conference in London in 1948 not only called for the convening of the Assembly but also produced a list of criteria which the Military Governors were to use to determine whether or not to approve the constitution. Indeed, they rejected the first draft in March 1949, while granting approval to a revised version soon after in May.

For their part, the delegates mostly shared the worries of the Allies. The bitter memory of Weimar never far from their minds, they wrote into the Basic Law numerous protections against democratic support of anti-democratic personalities and policies. Their many, often ingenious devices – the civil

33

liberties guaranteed to all humans in, as opposed to just citizens of, the FRG; the constructive vote of no confidence; the appointed President with limited powers; the independent judiciary; the Agency for the Protection of the Constitution – are too well known to review here. The important point is that the Basic Law and the government it authorized became imbued with a cynical spirit of protecting the Germans against themselves – a commitment the Germans refer to as 'vigilant democracy' (*streitbare Demokratie*). Georg-August Zinn, Social Democratic Minister-President of Hesse, articulated the prevailing sense of distrust in the Constituent Assembly when he told the body: 'We cannot afford to rely on the masses.'[41] Nor did they, for they chose not to put the Basic Law to the people via a referendum for ratification. But perhaps nothing better captures the drafters' fear of their compatriots than the so-called 'eternity clause' of the Basic Law. Article 79 makes forever unamendable the clauses concerning civil rights and the federal character of the republic.[42]

Many students of the Basic Law have rightly pointed to the paradox inherent in Article 79, indeed in the whole process of drafting the document under Allied direction. West German democracy is at heart an undemocratic democracy, an imposed democracy.[43] But this paradox bothered few back in 1949. Given the horrors of the Nazi regime, it seemed perfectly consistent to force the Germans to be free.

It was not long before the leaders of the infant republic began to force themselves to be free. Konrad Adenauer, Chancellor from 1949 to 1963, is usually credited with having

41 Quoted in Peter Merkle, *The Origins of the West German Republic* (New York: Oxford University Press, 1963), p. 81.

42 'The authors of the basic law seem to have dreaded the people, for the constitution holds the people's power to a minimum.' Karl Jaspers, *The Future of Germany* (Chicago: University of Chicago Press, 1967), p. 3.

43 Kurt Sontheimer (*The Government of the Federal Republic of Germany*, p. 30) makes this point, as does Ulrich Preuss, 'Political Concepts of Order for Mass Society,' in *Observations on 'The Spiritual Situation of the Age,'* ed. Jürgen Habermas (Cambridge, Mass.: MIT Press, 1985), pp. 118–119.

won back the trust of the Allies by firmly anchoring the Federal Republic in Western waters. He oversaw the drafting of the Basic Law as President of the Constituent Assembly. He made sure, with the help of economics wizard Ludwig Erhard, that the Federal Republic developed a capitalist market economy with enough growth and prosperity to sustain a large middle class. He also energetically supported the free market throughout West Europe by joining the EEC. He convinced his own people that rearmament was necessary and the French that it was not threatening and paved the way for West Germany's entrance into NATO. Eager to prove himself a worthy ally, Adenauer took up the banner against communism. In his foreign policy, he refused to recognize the GDR and cut off all communications with other countries that did recognize the East Germans. Domestically, he accused communists of working for Moscow and made them appear as dangerous as neo-Nazis (hence, the common expression of the time *'braun gleich rot'*). It is no wonder that both the Socialist Reich Party and the Communist Party were outlawed in the 1950s. These policies and others convinced the Allies that Germany was a dependable friend.

The Allies liked Adenauer's style as much as his policies; for the Chancellor too distrusted the German masses. He sought to keep political participation and opposition to a minimum. Although he never infringed the basic rules of parliamentary government, he exploited his constitutional and political power to gain strict obedience from his supporters in the cabinet, the *Bundestag*, and the CDU. 'Chancellor democracy' is an apt label for the Adenauer era, given his paternalistic and authoritarian style of leadership.

In Adenauer's chancellor democracy, the general public played a minor role. Deeply pessimistic about the capacities of the German people to measure up to the demands of democratic citizenship, he wanted their support but not their involvement. In short, Adenauer wanted to govern and he did not want the parliament, his party, his cabinet ministers, or the public to bother him while he went about his business. His message to the German public was, in essence: 'Go about your private affairs, rebuild your lives, concentrate on regaining and improving your economic position, and leave the politics to me.'[44]

Adenauer embodied the German paradox – a committed democrat willing to use essentially undemocratic means to protect democracy.

Adenauer's success lay in recognizing what his people most wanted (needed?): they were primarily interested in putting their shattered private lives back together. Politics was secondary. Adenauer spared them further disasters, political, economic, and military; he delivered peace, security, and prosperity. His effective policies spread confidence in and legitimacy for democracy by proving that it could work; that it could bring happiness and harmony and not the hardship and turmoil of the Weimar Republic. The people rewarded him at the polls, giving his coalition electoral hegemony in the 1950s and early 1960s.

Adenauer deserves credit for forging a broad and lasting consensus regarding the form and direction of the new republic. He also left his opponents (the SPD) with no choice but to concur. In 1959 in Godesberg, the Social Democrats renounced their vision of a different kind of republic (socialist) and agreed that NATO, capitalism, and liberal democracy were good for all Germans, even workers. This forged the stable two-and-a-half party system which since then has held German politics on a moderate course. Thus, when the magic of the economic miracle wore off and West Germany slumped into recession in 1966, the two large moderate parties formed the grand coalition to fight off the scare of a resurgent neo-Nazi party. There appeared this time to be real support among leaders for democracy. West Germany was

44 David Conradt, *The German Polity* (New York: Longman, 1989), p. 157.

not a 'fair-weather democracy' which could only survive in prosperous times; Bonn was indeed not Weimar.

Or was it? Anxiety over the fragility of West German democracy continued to emanate from the intelligentsia. In 1966, Karl Jaspers made the bestseller list with *Wohin treibt die Bundesrepublik?* (Where is the Federal Republic Heading?). His answer: 'toward dictatorship.' In the planned grand coalition he detected an emerging 'oligarchy of the parties' which would suffocate meaningful opposition and debate. In the proposed emergency laws he spotted a creeping authoritarianism. And in the citizenry, which docilely endured these trends, he saw the old German penchant for obsequiousness.

Centuries of authoritarian government have left us Germans with a residue of half-conscious attitudes which remain strong to this day. There is respect for the government as such, no matter what kind, no matter how established. There is the need to worship the state in its representative politicians, as substitutes for king and emperor. There is the subject's awe for authority in all its forms, down to the lowliest clerk behind an office window; there is the readiness to obey blindly, the confidence that the government will do right. . . . In short, the way we feel about our government is often still the way a subject feels; it is not the democratic attitude of a free citizen.[45]

In Jaspers' view, the Federal Republic had the trappings of democracy – constitution, parliament, elections – but absent was the spirit, the ethos. Germans were just going through the motions; they were not true believers.

This position turned into something of a creed in the 1960s for the critics of the *status quo*. Jaspers was the best-known critic but by no means the only or first one. In 1959, Gabriel Almond and Sidney Verba published *The Civic Culture*, in

45 Karl Jaspers, *The Future of Germany* (Chicago: University of Chicago Press, 1967), pp. 22–23.

37

which they concluded from extensive survey research that West Germany lacked the basic democratic political culture present in Britain and the United States. Britons and Americans exhibited high levels of system affect (pride in their democratic government), of civic confidence (belief that they as individuals could and should influence the government), of social trust and partisanship (faith in others and tolerance for differing opinions), and of informal participatory culture (desire to get involved in decision-making in the family, school, workplace, church, etc.). By contrast, Germans had little pride in their new government, desire or need to get involved in politics, faith in or tolerance for other citizens, and little inclination to influence decisions in various public and private groups. German political culture was instrumental rather than principled, pessimistic rather than optimistic, and hierarchical rather than participatory – all characteristics that could endanger democracy.

> Though the formal institutions of democracy exist in Germany and though there is a well-developed political infrastructure – a system of political parties and pressure groups – the underlying set of political attitudes that would regulate the operation of these institutions in a democratic direction is missing.[46]

Bracher echoed Almond and Verba when insisting that the key issue for the Federal Republic was 'whether the West German democracy shows itself to be a social and spiritual way of life [Lebensform] and not just a formal constitutional construction.'[47] Sontheimer used virtually the same words in wondering whether democracy in Germany was 'our way of life' (Lebensform) or merely 'our form of government' (Staatsform).[48]

46 G. Almond and S. Verba, *The Civic Culture* (Princeton: Princeton University Press, 1963), p. 496.

47 Bracher, *Deutschland zwischen Demokratie und Diktatur*, p. 136.

48 Sontheimer, *Antidemokratisches Denken*, p. 400.

Why did such skepticism persist despite nearly two decades of stable democracy? Obviously, events like the *Spiegel* affair, policies like the emergency laws, and personalities like Adenauer played a part in this relentless self-scrutiny. But the memory of Weimar particularly vexed intellectuals. For unlike Italy or Spain, where fascism came to power through force or the threat thereof, in Germany, Hitler became Chancellor through democratic means. Hence, a well-functioning democracy was not necessarily sufficient safeguard against authoritarianism. Something deeper, surer was needed. Nor did the reigning structural functionalist paradigm soothe anxiety. Its notion of a German pathology against liberalism gave the impression of a dormant virus always capable of revival. In this environment it was virtually impossible to convince the republic's caretakers that their patient was cured.

Willy Brandt capitalized on these worries. In 1969, he campaigned for Chancellor with the slogan 'Dare More Democracy.' Once Chancellor, he declared: 'We are not at the end of our democracy, we are only just beginning.'[49] The young leader promised a program of democratization that would reach every institution and person in the land. Brandt attacked the hierarchical nature of West German society and politics by pressing for equality of results rather than just opportunity through an expanded welfare state (for example, the Federal Education Promotion Act in 1971 or the Pension Reform Act of 1972). He also wanted to transform traditionally deferential citizens into 'mature citizens' (*mündige Bürger*) who both knew *and* exercised their rights. He welcomed increased political participation and worked to widen access to decision-making circles in other institutions (Law on the Framework of Higher Education and the Works Organization Act in 1971). Democratization also involved promoting greater tolerance for diversity and

49 In Klaus von Beyme (ed.), *Die grossen Regierungserklärungen der deutschen Kanzler von Adenauer bis Schmidt* (Munich: Hauser, 1979), p. 281.

non-conformity. The hope was to make room for a variety of different lifestyles to co-exist in a pluralist society.

Brandt restored the faith in progress punctured by the war. He represented a new optimistic generation which no longer had to content itself with disaster avoidance and could now strive to improve and perfect West Germany into a model society. In politics, this signaled a shift from merely defending the institutions of democracy from a few anti-democratic parties to engendering personal commitment among citizens to the spirit of democracy. The notion of 'vigilant democracy' thus acquired a much more aggressive meaning, transforming from prevention to proselytization, from defense to offense. The democratizing mission changed from exorcizing demons to converting souls.[50]

Helmut Schmidt deflated the progressive optimism of the Brandt era when he entered the Chancellory in 1974. His technocratic style of leadership seemed to value pragmatism at the expense of idealism. Reeling from the oil shock of 1973, Schmidt concentrated more on holding down inflation than on unemployment. In his stern response to RAF terrorism in 1977, he appeared to prefer order to change. And with the installation of Pershing cruise missiles on German soil in 1982, he seemed to sell out Brandt's vision of international harmony to Reagan's focus on hostility.

Actually though, Schmidt did not so much reverse Brandt's reforms as cease to intensify them. For instance, Schmidt did not expand the welfare state but he did maintain it so that most Germans could count on a modicum of material security. If he failed to implore his people to become more involved in politics, he surely did nothing to stop the blossoming of hundreds of grassroots movements (*Bürgerinitiative*) in the 1970s. Schmidt stayed the basic course of his predecessors toward becoming a dependable Western republic. But by his time, dramatic turns were no longer necessary.

50 We can see this change in the *Radikalenerlass* of 1972, which shifted the emphasis away from banning whole parties to testing individuals' personal commitment to democracy.

This certainly seemed to be borne out by research into German political culture. The massive surveys of German political attitudes started during the occupation continued into the 1970s. But the analysts began finding something new. To quote the title of one prominent study, they found a *Germany Transformed*. Survey research showed that as the generation socialized after the war gradually replaced the older generation, so too did a democratic political culture supplant the traditional authoritarian one. West Germans started scoring as high or higher than other Western publics on the '*Demokratie-skala*.' Astonishingly, they seemed to be more Western than their Western mentors. Bracher felt justified in declaring Germany a 'post-national democracy.'[51] Jürgen Habermas contended that *Verfassungspatriotismus* had replaced traditional nationalistic patriotism.[52] Perhaps Kendall Baker, Russell Dalton, and Kai Hildebrandt described the transformation best:

> In just three decades the Federal Republic has experienced a massive transformation of political and social norms and values: from a traditional social order and a war-ravaged economy to a progressive advanced industrial society; from a country plagued by severe conflicts and cleavages to a highly stable, integrated society in which the democratic political system constructed after World War II seems to enjoy substantial legitimacy. Thus the Federal Republic exemplifies – possibly accentuates – the general development of modern Western democracies.[53]

The Allied project was complete. A new liberal nation-state had come of age. Schmidt sensed his people's achievement

51 'Politik und Zeitgeist. Tendenzen der siebziger Jahre,' in *Republik im Wandel 1969–1974*, eds K. Bracher, W. Jaeger, and W. Link (Stuttgart: Deutsche Verlag-Anstalt, 1986), p. 402.
52 'Einleitung,' in *Stichworte zur geistigen Situation der Zeit*, ed. J. Habermas (Frankfurt: Suhrkamp, 1979), pp. 7–35.
53 K. Baker, R. Dalton, and K. Hildebrandt, *Germany Transformed* (Cambridge, Mass.: Harvard University Press, 1981), p. 9.

and centered his 1976 campaign around the slogan '*Modell Deutschland.*' Germans could be proud, he was saying, for their country had become a nation to be admired instead of abhorred.

Yet, just as the intelligentsia were becoming confident about their polity and people, they were forced to take notice of a large foreign element in their midst: migrants. These newcomers would pose grave challenges to the republic. In the first place, the migrants had not, like the West Germans, been subjected to a rigorous campaign of democratization. Most came from and therefore grew up in authoritarian societies. Second, would the West Germans treat the aliens with the tolerance and equality demanded of sincere liberals or lapse back into bigotry? It was one thing to tolerate fellow Germans of different stripes, quite another to tolerate non-Germans, even non-Christians. And finally, if racism revived, would, could, the West German leaders protect the migrants and with them the republic's liberal constitution and identity?

3

LIBERALIZING *AUSLÄNDERPOLITIK* 1969–1982

[P]ast measures have clearly been too colored by the priority of market perspectives, while the equally important social and political considerations appeared unimportant. . . . The migrants who wish to stay . . . must be made the offer of unrestricted, lasting integration.

(Heinz Kühn, Federal Commissioner for Aliens)

INTRODUCTION

Large-scale migration of non-Germans into the Federal Republic startled the West Germans. On the one hand, it caught them by surprise, beginning as a tiny trickle of temporary laborers in the 1950s, growing to a steady stream of permanent workers in the 1960s, and swelling into a mighty river of immigrants – wives, children, grandparents, cousins – that seemed to flood the nation in the 1970s. On the other hand, it evoked the bitterest memories of the past. For it was in the wanton persecution of minorities that Germans had most disgraced themselves. A large minority presence, reaching 5 per cent of the population by the early 1970s, haunted Germans like an unwanted temptation to fall back into bad habits.

But temptation affords a chance for relapse *or* reaffirmation. If we give into it, our recovery is incomplete; but if we resist, we feel all the more fully cured. Social Democratic

43

governments of the 1970s sensed the danger of a nationalist revival in response to the migrant problem and committed the nation to a liberal *Ausländerpolitik* (policies governing aliens). The cornerstone of this reformed policy was integration (*Integration*) which ultimately aimed at the realization of fully equal rights and opportunities for migrants in social, economic, legal, and political matters. The program moved West Germany further in the direction of a multicultural society based on liberal rather than nationalist principles and therefore strengthened the Germans' image of themselves as a modern, tolerant, democratic people.

But the reformers did not stop there. They detected in the migrants the same ailment that had once afflicted the Germans: pathological fear of rapid, inevitable change. With the new-found zeal and self-confidence of a recovering alcoholic who, once cured, pledges to save other drunks, Social Democrats structured integration so as to resocialize migrants to the enlightened values of the modern liberal democratic society in which they now lived. The campaign was closely analogous to and profoundly informed by the Germans' own experience of having been integrated into the Western community after the war. Only now, the Germans were the liberalizers, the migrants the ones to be liberalized. And this helped further to convince leaders that they had made an irreversible conversion to Western liberalism.

By the end of the 1970s, the Federal Republic had become thickly entangled in the migrant problem. West Germany not only relied on migrants economically, to work the jobs no one else wanted, but also politically, to relieve West Germany from the heavy burden of its own shameful self-image.

DISCOVERING THE PROBLEM

Non-German migration to Germany began in 1955. As the economic miracle continued to work its wonders, increased demand for labor could no longer be met by the 12 million

German refugees from the east. In addition, resumed conscription promised to take many of the ablest workers out of the factories. Faced with the prospect of full employment (and thus strengthened labor unions), the Adenauer administration signed a treaty with Rome allowing it to recruit Italians to work in West Germany. Similar treaties followed, with Spain and Greece in 1960, Turkey in 1961, and Yugoslavia in 1968. The number of migrant workers steadily grew (from roughly 80,000 in 1955 to 1.3 million in 1966), and foreigners came to form an integral part of the labor force in several key industries (metal, textile, auto, fishing, hotel, and catering).

Despite their absorption into the economy, few Germans took much note or care of the foreign laborers. After all, they never made up more than 3 per cent of the population. Furthermore, they mostly kept to themselves, typically housed in barracks at or near the workplace. Most importantly, the foreigners were considered temporary or 'guestworkers' who would soon return to their homelands. Surely, the Adenauer administration chose the label '*Gastarbeiter*' to avoid the ugly term '*Fremdarbeiter*' used in the Third Reich. But the term also conveyed the original goal of *Ausländerpolitik*. The administration's 'rotation principle' (*Rotationsprinzip*) stipulated that migrants would be allowed to stay in Germany two or three years before being rotated back home and replaced by a new cohort. In this way, Bonn hoped it could spread the prosperity of the German economic miracle to less developed economies in southern Europe, in the meantime promoting further European harmony and integration.

First in the late 1960s and early 1970s, West Germans began to discover the problems, and not just the benefits, associated with large-scale migration. And this happened because the character and consequences of the migration changed markedly after the recession of 1966–1967. When the recession passed, employers pressed government not only to recruit more foreign workers but also to let them stay longer. Firms reasoned that their investment in foreign laborers only really paid off after a year or two of initial training. It therefore made no (economic) sense to send them back home after two or three years, as had been the practice under the rotation principle. The Ministry of Labor responded by abandoning the rotation principle and granting long-term, even unlimited work permits to practically all migrants who had extended contracts with their employers. The average length of stay of the migrants steadily increased, and the temporary-sounding label of 'guestworkers' came to sound more and more like a misnomer.[1]

This new strategy dramatically altered the demographics of migration. Foreign workers, who now planned to stay for some time or for good, understandably wished to bring their families to their sides; and they did. In 1961, there had been over 100,000 non-working foreign dependants in West Germany; by 1971, there were more than a million. Thirty-five per cent of the guestworkers were not workers at all, but spouses and children. In addition, the ethnic make-up of the foreign population changed during those years. Until 1967, Italians represented the single largest national group among migrants; but from 1967, Turkish migration took off, growing from roughly 200,000 to 900,000 between 1967 and 1973.[2] Now Turks, usually considered most different from Germans, made up the largest ethnic group. '*Das Ausländerproblem ist ein türkisches Problem*' became a common expression.

As policy-makers felt increasingly compelled to change the official label for migrants from 'guestworkers' to 'foreign workers and their family members' ('*ausländische Arbeitnehmer und ihre Familienangehörigen*'), they could not help but notice the grave social consequences of migration. Foreigners

1 Uli Bielefeld, *Inländische Ausländer* (Frankfurt: Campus, 1988), p. 115.
2 For a nice statistical summary of migration, see Jürgen Zander, 'Ausländer in Deutschland – Einführung in die Probleme,' in *Ausländer in Deutschland – Für eine gemeinsame Zukunft*, ed. Heiner Geissler (Munich: Günter Olzog, 1982), pp. 14–35.

who during the first decade of migration had been willing to live with their fellow countrymen in spartan barracks at the factory were now appearing at public agencies seeking cheap, adequate housing for an entire family. Welfare workers who had earlier attended to the modest needs of mainly young, healthy, resourceful male migrants were now faced with foreigners of all ages, sexes, and dispositions in need of a wide array of social services. And the schools, once comfortably homogeneous, were now having to absorb pupils with different nationalities, languages, races, and religions. Between 1965 and 1975, the number of foreign pupils in German schools increased tenfold. In other words, what had begun as a rather limited and purely beneficial economic phenomenon mushroomed into a full-blown social problem. Or as Max Frisch so tellingly put it in 1971: 'We asked for workers, and human beings showed up.'

The migrant problem was no longer an issue which could be neglected as peripheral. Nor did Brandt's administration, with its promise of far-reaching social reform, wish to ignore it. The National Labor Office carried out the first nationwide study of the working and living conditions of foreigners in 1968; it was ordered in 1972 to repeat the survey of 14,000 aliens.[3] Although these studies stood as the most comprehensive, many others were either conducted or commissioned by various federal ministries and by *Land* and local governments acutely affected by migration.[4] In addition, several independent studies came out which caught the eye of public officials.[5] They could catch their eye because

---

3 *Repräsentativ-untersuchung '68* and *Repräsentativ-untersuchung '72* (Nuremberg: Institut für Arbeitsmarkt und Berufsforschung, 1969 and 1973).

4 See, for instance, Ursula Mehrländer, *Beschäftigung ausländischer Arbeitnehmer in der Bundesrepublik Deutschland unter spezieller Berücksichtigung von Nordrhein-Westfalen* (Opladen: Westdeutscher Verlag, 1969); or Maria Borris, *Ausländische Arbeiter in einer Grossstadt* (Frankfurt: Europäische Verlagsanstalt, 1973).

5 Marios Nikolinakos, *Politische Ökonomie der Gastarbeiterfrage. Migration und Kapitalismus* (Reinbek bei Hamburg: Rowohlt, 1973).

most governments had established special migration task forces like the one first formed in the Federal Ministry of Labor in 1970 to evaluate the old and propose a new *Ausländerpolitik*.

What these early investigations found proved disturbing. The Federal Republic was forming an underclass of non-Germans systematically underprivileged in economic, social, and political life. At work, migrants invariably held the unskilled, lowest-paying positions. They were often subject to arbitrary dismissal without protection from German labor unions. At home, foreigners were victimized by crafty landlords who forced them to pay exorbitant rents for seedy, overcrowded housing in the worst parts of town. In 1971–1972, for instance, only a quarter of migrants' apartments had central heating; only half had a bathroom. When they sought to move from these ghettos, migrants ran into discriminatory practices designed to keep them out of 'German' neighborhoods. At school, foreign pupils were failing in disproportionate numbers, nearly half not even graduating from the *Hauptschule* (high school). High attrition was blamed on a 1964 policy of the Standing Conference of State Ministers of Education which, rather than designing measures to address the special needs of foreign children, ordered that they be absorbed into normal German classes as quickly as possible.

Before the law, too, migrants were at a disadvantage. It shocked many Germans to learn that until 1965 foreigners were subject to the Aliens Police Decree of 1938, which tied the residence permit to whether their 'residence in the Empire's territory offers assurance that they are worthy of the hospitality shown them' (Section 1). The new Aliens Law of 1965 offered little improvement. Section 2 stipulated that the foreigner can be granted a residence permit only if he 'does not injure the interests of the Federal Republic of Germany.' Section 6 permitted the state to restrict the political activity of foreigners if it 'endangers the free democratic order.' Moreover, the law left to bureaucratic discretion what it meant by to 'injure' Germany's interests or 'endanger' its political order. Reports documented countless cases in which police abused their power to intimidate foreigners, denying or canceling residence permits for such things as breaking contracts, accepting social assistance, organizing a migrant association, or even receiving a minor traffic violation.[6]

A new picture of migration was emerging. West Germany no longer had a few 'guests' trying to make a fast buck; it had a growing substratum of second-class citizens. Ernst Klee, writing a book in 1971 on migrants in all of Europe, seemed justified in calling them 'Europe's niggers.'[7] To make matters worse, studies like Klee's forecasted trouble. Taken together, these fact-finding reports painted a scenario of impending civil strife potentially as disruptive as the civil rights crisis in the USA. The economy was undeniably dependent on migrants. Core industries had come to rely on foreign labor as a cheap way to expand production without having to make major capital investments into new technologies. Moreover, German workers, who moved up into well-paid skilled jobs precisely because migrants were available, could not be expected to return to the less desirable, albeit essential positions filled by foreigners. The Federation of German Employers' Associations reported in 1973 that a large foreign labor force was simply a given for the foreseeable future.[8]

Yet, whoever thought the second generation of migrants would remain docile and quiescent like the first was mistaken. Studies found that adult migrants used their countrymen back home as a reference group; and by this comparison life in Germany seemed pretty good. But their children raised in Germany would likely compare their lot with German youth and find it wanting. Relative deprivation, to

---

6 See Hans Heinz Heldmann, *Ausländerrecht. Disziplinarordnung für die Minderheit* (Darmstadt: Hermann Luchterhand, 1974).

7 Ernst Klee, *Die Neger Europas* (Düsseldorf: Patmos Verlag, 1971).

8 Bundesvereinigung der Deutschen Arbeitgeberverbände, *Kurz-Nachrichten-Dienst* (November 20, 1973).

use the social scientific jargon, would give way to social frustration and culminate in either individual or collective deviant behavior. Greater demands on the state from migrants would in turn trigger an aggressive backlash from German nationals which, if accompanied by a recession, could get ugly.[9] The kind of ethnic and religious hatred which once plagued Weimar could return to menace Bonn. *Bonn war vielleicht doch Weimar.*

The events of 1973 confirmed these prognoses. OPEC's embargo sent oil prices spiraling upward and the economy downward. With layoffs and wage restraint imminent, labor unrest erupted. In the wave of wildcat strikes that swept the nation, migrants played a leading role. In the most dramatic incident (at the Ford factory in Cologne), Turkish workers seized control of the plant, refused to let IG Metall represent them, and negotiated directly with management until they were forcibly ejected by police. Gone was the image of the servile guestworker. The nation experienced first-hand how migrants could significantly disrupt production in key industries. Concern also mounted over the strain foreign workers and their families would put on a welfare state already overtaxed by recession. Could Germany afford to employ and care for a large migrant population when it could hardly do the same for its own citizens? Xenophobia spread as many Germans felt their country under siege by outsiders. The popular weekly *Der Spiegel* expressed the nation's common anxiety in one of its lead articles that year entitled 'The Turkish Invasion.'

THE NATIONALIST SOLUTION

The dramatic events of 1973 prompted a swift response from government. Bonn reverted to what it knew best. During the previous recession, it had managed to reduce the number of

9 Hans-Joachim Hoffmann-Nowotny, *Soziologie des Fremdarbeiterproblem* (Stuttgart: Enke, 1973).

migrants by 300,000 with tighter regulations. In June, the government announced its intention to 'consolidate' the foreign population. On November 23, the Ministry of Labor decreed a halt to the recruitment of foreign workers from outside the EEC. Other restrictive measures followed. The Ministries of Labor and Interior collaborated on a campaign to revoke work and residence permits from migrants who fell back on social assistance. Bonn also ordered that work permits would be forbidden for migrants' children who entered the country after November 30, 1974 (the so-called *Stichtagregelung*). In the following year, migrants lost their freedom of movement. They were legally barred from taking up residence in certain urban districts designated 'overly burdened' (*'überbelastet'*) by too high a percentage (12 per cent) of alien inhabitants. In 1978, the age at which children of migrants could no longer legally emigrate to Germany was reduced from 20 to 18. In 1981, it was further reduced to 16 (except in Bremen).[10]

These restrictive measures suggested enduring nationalism. They put *German* interests first. Migrants were only welcome so long as they enhanced the *German* economy. In official language: the 'extent [of foreign employment] is to be determined according to the development of the labor market and the economy.'[11] Furthermore, sacred liberal principles – equality before the law, freedom of movement, the sanctity of the family, tolerance for diversity – were jettisoned when it came to migrants. The much-heralded *human* rights of the first section of the Basic Law appeared in fact to be *German* rights. Finally, authoritarian practices in the form of unchecked police power were countenanced in the name of protecting the national interest. These policies seemed to have much more in common with Adenauer's

10 For a detailed account of measures taken to reduce the number of foreigners, see Knuth Dohse, *Ausländische Arbeiter und bürgerlicher Staat* (Königstein: Anton Hain, 1981).
11 'Grundsätze zur Eingliederung ausländischer Arbeitnehemer,' *Bundesarbeitsblatt* 4 (1970): 281.

pragmatic, autocratic style than with Brandt's idealistic, liberalizing aims. The nationalist *Konsolidierungspolitik* of the mid-1970s could stand as an important counter-example to the 'Germany transformed' thesis which surfaced at that time; could, that is, if a liberal *Integrationspolitik* had not simultaneously emerged to challenge and ultimately eclipse the nationalist response.

THE LIBERAL SOLUTION

Calls for integration were first heard in the late 1960s and then crescendoed in the 1970s. Integrationists were typically those who worked closely with migrants – church and social workers who helped them and scholars who studied them. They were able effectively to influence policy because many were assigned to the various *Ausländerkommissionen* in the federal and *Land* ministries. They consistently defended migrants' rights and attacked policies bent on repatriating them. Statements like the following from the Catholic Church were made by many other organizations, in particular the Evangelical Church of Germany and the Worker Welfare Association:

> A consolidation or reduction of the number of foreign workers is permissible only if it results from a decrease in new recruitment and in no way from a forced repatriation of those already here. . . . The alien should be granted a right to a long-term residency . . . through clearly outlined conditions.[12]

These advocates for migrants argued that Germany had to own up to the fact that it would long need and attract massive numbers of migrants. The solution to the problem lay in acknowledging their permanence and integrating them out of the margin into the mainstream of society. Their demands were heeded, and *Integrationspolitik* was adopted

12 Synode der Bistümer, 'Die ausländischen Arbeitnehmer – eine Frage an die Kirche und die Gesellschaft,' *Synode Heft* 2 (1974): 23.

along with *Konsolidierungspolitik*. On April 22, 1972, the Coordinating Committee 'Foreign Workers' in the Ministry of Labor published the government's first major statement in favor of integration with its report 'Principles and Measures for the Integration of Foreign Workers and their Families.' Many definitions of and blueprints for integration were subsequently floated inside and outside government. All, however, shared three key components:

1 recognition of migration as a permanent phenomenon;
2 a demand for full equality for foreigners socially, economically, legally, and politically; and
3 a plea for tolerance for diversity, for acceptance of the Federal Republic as a multi-cultural society.

Integration found a cozy place in the reformist agenda of the Brandt era. If every walk of German life was to be thoroughly democratized as Brandt had promised, then surely *Ausländerpolitik* had to be included. It was 'in' to be pro-integration in the 1970s, just as it was to be pro-peace, pro-environment, pro-women.

In their opposition to consolidation, integrationists were aided by the migrants (who proved adept at circumventing restrictive measures) and by the courts (who struck down the measures as unconstitutional). Some policies simply backfired. Thus the *Stichtagregelung* led thousands of migrants to bring their children to Germany before the November 30, 1974 deadline. Many migrants got around the statute lowering the maximum age at which their children could join them in Germany by falsifying or merely conveniently losing birth certificates. The Germans quickly learned just how hard it was to plug all the holes in the border. Nor should we overlook the higher birthrates among foreigners. Migrants were typically having 13–15 per cent of the babies annually while representing only 6–7 per cent of the total population. Through the rest of the 1970s, the total number of migrants remained constant at about 4 million; by 1982, when the SPD was ousted from the ruling coalition, the number was 4.6 million.

The courts – that most *verfassungspatriotisch* of institutions – chipped away at the pillars of *Konsolidierungspolitik*. As early as July 18, 1973, the Federal Constitutional Court set a liberal tone which would govern the review of migration policies. On that date, the court declared that the 'free development of the personality' (*'freie Entfaltung der Persönlichkeit'*) guaranteed in Article 2 applied to both aliens and citizens. Any policies which violated this basic *human* right would therefore be considered unconstitutional. In 1976, state administrative courts began declaring unconstitutional the statutes in various cities barring foreigners from moving into 'overly burdened' districts; by 1979, the measure was practiced nowhere. In 1976, a court in Giessen ordered the National Labor Office to award an alien unemployment insurance despite the fact that she had no work permit.

With these decisions and others, the courts sent a strong message to policy-makers. The latter knew harsh measures would not pass muster. Consequently, they themselves took steps to avoid or rescind highly restrictive statutes. In 1973, for example, the Ministry of Labor stated that it would not 'forcibly terminate' (*'zwangsweise beenden'*) a migrant's stay in Germany. In that same year, Bonn also rejected a proposal emanating from Bavaria to place a ceiling on the number of foreigners permitted in Germany. The much contested *Stichtag* for foreign youths was once lengthened and then done away with altogether in 1979. A year earlier, the Federal government had passed the Stabilization Statute (*Verfestigungsregel*). This decree clearly outlined the requirements for receiving the unlimited residence permit and the residence entitlement, thus drastically limiting the bureaucratic discretion which had been abused in the past. From 1978 to 1984, the number of foreigners possessing one or the other long-term permits rose from 388, 254 to 1,3337,694.[13]

As consolidation proved ineffective, integration gathered

13 *Ausländerpolitik* (Bonn: Bundesminister für Arbeit und Sozialordnung, 1985), p. 15.

momentum. Originally, the two strategies were to work hand in hand. Consolidation would reduce the number of foreigners, and integration would give the small number of those who chose to stay equal rights and opportunities. But when the numbers failed to fall, integration grew into a much larger task than first conceived. The Schmidt administration did not shirk this responsibility. In 1976, a special *Bund-Länder Kommission* was formed and charged to draft a comprehensive proposal for *Ausländerpolitik*. Its 'Suggestions for the Further Development of a Comprehensive Conception for Policy on Foreign Employment,' published the following year, acknowledged that a large migrant population was a given for the indefinite future and urged the government to intensify its programs of integration. Bonn took the advice and increased its expenditures on integration from DM15,063,000 in 1973 to DM30,676,000 in 1978, to DM84,567,000 in 1983.[14] But the greatest victory for integration came in 1978 with the creation of the Office of the Commissioner for Foreign Workers. Well-respected Heinz Kühn, former Minister-President of North Rhine-Westphalia, was appointed the new Commissioner (*Beauftragter*). His first report, dubbed the 'Kühn Memorandum,' immediately became the government's centerpiece document, its guiding philosophy, on *Ausländerpolitik*.

It was a decidedly liberal memorandum. Kühn called for 'a consequential policy of integration' with these features:

- recognition of *de facto* immigration
- major intensification of integrative measures
- abolition of all segregating measures
- opportunity for youths for unhindered access to jobs and job training
- a legal right to naturalization for youths born and raised in the Federal Republic
- general reassessment of the rights of foreigners and of the requirements for naturalization with the goal of greater

14 Ibid., p. 39.

    legal security and stronger consideration of the legitimate
    special interests of foreign workers and their families
- improvement of their political rights through the granting
  of local voting rights after extended residence
- improvement of problem-oriented social assistance.[15]

Kühn delighted integrationists. For he not only went on to
spell out in great detail what should be done to achieve each
of these goals, he also emphasized that integration could not
be preached or practiced as assimilation. 'Forced Germanization' ('*Zwangsgermanisierung*') was out of the question
because the migrants deserved 'a guaranteed opportunity to
preserve their identity.'[16]

Kühn sparked an integration fever in the land. The Ministry of Labor followed up the memorandum with the outline
of a massive campaign for 'The Integration of the Second
Generation of Foreigners.' *Land* and city governments either
initiated or expanded hundreds of integration efforts –
language courses, vocational programs, special curricula,
childcare, counseling, cultural exhibitions, research grants,
migrant advisory councils. Perhaps the most ambitious –
and most liberal – in this spate of programs was the decision,
first taken by North Rhine-Westphalia but later by several
other *Länder*, to offer Islamic religious instruction to Muslim
pupils in the public schools parallel to Christian instruction
for Catholics and Protestants. The Germans had truly come
a long way. For so long, they had tried so hard to erase ethno-
religious minorities, most notably Jews and Poles, from the
land. They now appeared willing to bend over backwards to
help the 2 million Muslims living there to preserve their faith
in the diaspora.

Liberalism had triumphed. Integration was progressing.
By 1980, 54 per cent of foreigners who married in Germany

15 Kühn, 'Stand und Weiterentwicklung der Integration der ausländischen
    Arbeitnehmer und ihrer Familien in der Bundesrepublik Deutschland,'
    reprinted in *Gastarbeiter oder Einwanderer*, ed. Karl-Heinz Meier-Braun
    (Frankfurt: Ullstein, 1980), p. 30.
16 Ibid., p.46.

married a German (compared to 41 per cent in 1971). The number of migrant workers organized in German unions had jumped from 25 per cent in 1974 to 33.6 per cent in 1982. Turkish workers were better organized than Germans (48 per cent to 40 per cent)! Foreign pupils who entered German schools in the first grade were by the end of the 1970s performing at a level equal to their German classmates.[17] By no means, however, had all the goals of the liberal *Integrationspolitik* been achieved. Migrants suffered higher levels of unemployment than Germans. By the end of the recession of 1980–1981, 8.2 per cent of foreigners were registered as unemployed, only 5.5 per cent of Germans.[18] Fully equal political rights had not been granted. Migrants could not vote in official elections at any level. The naturalization process, lengthy, difficult, and expensive, continued to discourage migrants from becoming German citizens, as did Bonn's refusal to accept dual citizenship. The Federal Republic continued to record the lowest rate of immigrant naturalization in Europe.[19] Nor did all aspects of nationalistic *Konsolidierungspolitik* disappear. Bonn stubbornly maintained that the Federal Republic was not a 'land of immigration' ('*Einwanderungsland*') and refused to lift the ban on recruiting foreign workers. But this policy was tolerated largely because it was directed at foreigners outside the republic who wished to emigrate. Those inside, however, had to be treated in accordance with the liberal democratic values for which the republic stood. Generally speaking, nationalistic policies gave way to liberal ones. By the time he left office in 1982, Schmidt's administration, despite footdragging here and

17 Gert Hammer, 'Handlungssspielraum deutscher Ausländer-politik,' in Geissler, *Ausländer in Deutschland – Für eine gemeinsame Zukunft* (Munich: Günter Olzog, 1982), vol. I, pp. 15–51.
18 Margret Ladener-Malcher, 'Ausländer in der Arbeitswelt,' in ibid., p. 129.
19 See Kay Hailbronner, 'Citizenship and Nationhood in Germany,' in *Immigration and the Politics of Citizenship in Europe and North America*, ed. William Rogers Brubaker (Lanham: University Press of America, 1989), pp. 67–80.

backsliding there, had firmly placed West Germany's *Ausländerpolitik* on a liberal foundation.

CHANGING PLACES

But construing the campaign for integration as a mere *effect* of solidified liberalism obscures a crucial point: namely, that the liberalized *Ausländerpolitik* of the 1970s played a significant *causal* role in promoting liberalism (or at least confidence in it among elites). For integration, as it was conceptualized and practiced, enabled West German intellectuals to displace the negative image of themselves and their people inherited from the Second World War onto the foreigners. As a result, the migrants came out looking like the anti-democratic nationalists to be feared; the West Germans like good Western liberals to be admired. To put it differently, through *Integrationspolitik* the West Germans boosted themselves up into that esteemed category of 'Western' peoples from which they had long been excluded. But to get there they had to step on the backs of migrants.

Integration must be understood in the broader West European and Atlantic context. What West Germans knew of 'integration' they knew from their own experiences of integrating into the EEC and NATO. European integration was conceived out of respect for the inherent ethnic diversity of the continent. The architects of the EEC envisaged a single state for Western Europe, but not like the stereotypical nineteenth-century nation-state with an ethnically homogeneous citizenry. Accordingly, the Treaty of Paris stated as the primary aim of the European Coal and Steel Community: 'To create by establishing an economic community, the basis for a broader and deeper community among peoples long divided by bloody conflicts; and to lay the foundations for institutions which will give direction to a destiny henceforward shared.' Certainly, there was always talk of a single European consciousness forming in the distant future, but even this was to entail an appreciation for the rich diversity of the continent's peoples. No one expected a single ethnic group, say the French, to dominate the EEC and assimilate all the other nationalities. The same was true of other transnational organizations like the OECD, the Council of Europe, and NATO. Even in the latter, which the USA clearly dominated, no one demanded that the Germans stop being German and become American in order to gain membership. It was just this kind of vainglorious desire for national supremacy which was believed to have caused the two world wars.

No people was more painfully aware of this than the Germans. When it came to dealing with migrants, therefore, they steered clear of a policy of assimilation. Thus Kühn's insistence that integration could not involve Germanization was hardly unique; similar anti-assimilationist caveats appeared in practically every official statement on integration.[20] The idea of ethnic assimilation was simply alien to postwar Germans. On the one hand, they, like other Europeans, did not think of ethnicity as something one could choose, like a brand of cereal on a store shelf. One was simply born a German, Greek, or Turk and remained German, Greek, or Turkish for life. On the other hand, even if assimilation were possible, who in their right mind would want to become German? The Germans had the worst reputation in the whole of Europe; even Germans were ashamed of being German.

But if integration was not assimilation, what was it? Here too, the integrationists leaned on their experience with the rest of Europe. The idea of European integration reposed on three premises: first, that a truly modern industrial economy, in order to prosper, had to be much larger than the individual national economies of the countries of Western Europe; second, this meant that the different nations of Western Europe had to find a way to cooperate rather than compete with one

20 See *Vorschläge der Bund-Länder-Kommission zur Fortentwicklung einer umfassenden Konzeption der Ausländer-beschäftigungspolitik* (Bonn: Bundesministerium für Arbeit und Sozialordnung, 1977); or *Weiterentwicklung der Ausländerpolitik* (Bonn: Bundesministerium für Arbeit und Sozialordnung, 1980).

another; and, third, the foundation of this cooperation was to be the principles of liberal democracy and free-market economy. The latter premise, in turn, forged a common interest with the North Atlantic peoples of the United Kingdom and the United States in terms of defending the 'free world' against the communist bloc to the east.

But membership in the Western alliance involved one other critical dimension unique to the Germans. Whereas the leaders, France, Britain, and the United States, were all assumed to be fully modern societies with a mature liberal citizenry, West Germany was not. As discussed in Chapter 2, the Allies deliberately set out to liberalize West Germany in order to integrate it into the Western anti-communist alliance. And as we also saw, much of postwar West German politics centered on debating and assessing how much Germany had been transformed. Thus integration into the Western community did entail for Germans a change of identity. But it did not mean giving up their ethnic identity. As Chancellor Brandt had implied in his popular phrase 'Two states, one nation,' not even the division of Germany could destroy the ethnic unity of the German people. European integration involved rather a political and ethical transformation of conscience from a traditional, authoritarian to modern, liberal culture. In other words, the aim was not to de-Germanize, but to liberalize.

It was natural that Social Democrats would adopt this same liberalizing mentality when it came to integrating migrants into West German society. They had ridden into office in 1969 on the promise of completing the liberalization of the republic started but not finished by their Christian Democratic predecessors. This same promise, in turn, ideologically obligated the Social Democrats, once it was clear migrants were going to remain in Germany indefinitely, to devise an *Ausländerpolitik* based on liberal as opposed to nationalist distinctions between insiders and outsiders. We find, for instance, in the position papers on integration in the 1970s no talk of, say, Turkish migrants as a potentially irredentist minority, as was common with Poles in previous German regimes. Such concern made no sense not only because Germans and Turks were not vying for the same land, but also because they had been allies in recent wars. What did make sense was that Turks and other migrants moved to Germany because their homelands were 'developing countries' (*'Entwicklungsländer'*) with weak economies and few jobs, while West Germany was an 'industrial society' (*'Industriegesellschaft'*) with a strong economy and many jobs.[21]

Nor do we find even a hint of the kind of conspiracy theory once viciously employed against Jews. Jews had been stereotyped as especially adroit at maneuvering themselves into elite positions from which they secretly manipulated German economy and politics to serve the interests of international Jewry. But among the postwar migrants, there were no Jugoslav, Greek, or Spanish equivalents of Walther Rathenau at whom to point the finger. Official papers reiterated over and over that the migrants constituted an underprivileged 'subproletariat' working and living under miserable conditions. If the predominant view of Jews had been of an exceptionally able minority which could threaten Germans, the typical image of Turkish and other migrants was of the simple villager helpless and confused in a complex modern society.[22]

Even the roughly 2 million Muslim migrants did not worry officials, at least not as a threat to the Christian character of the nation. As already mentioned, Muslims were not pressured to deny or renounce their faith as many Jews had once been. Nor did the government undertake a systematic campaign to destroy Islam like Bismarck's *Kulturkampf* against Roman Catholicism. Officials acknowledged the migrants' constitutional right to free worship (Articles 3 and 4) as well as the state's obligation (Article 7) actively to assist

21 See *Konzept zur Beschäftigung ausländischer Arbeitnehmer* (Bonn: Sozialdemokratische Partei Deutschlands, 1975).
22 See Otto Neuloh, Güter Endruweit, and Hans Leo Kraemer, *Integration oder Rückkehr* (Bundesministerium für Arbeit und Sozialordnung, 1974).

large religious groups in the practice and pursuit of their faith. It was, in part, this highly *verfassungspatriotisch* attitude which gave rise to the campaign started in the late 1970s to provide Islamic religious education in the public schools.[23]

What most distinguished migrants from Germans, in the eyes of integrationists, was not their nationality, ethnicity, or religion, but their level of social and cultural development. Alongside the image of the migrants as an exploited, marginalized minority, emerged the equally widespread view of them as traditional, backward people living in a modern industrial society. Transplanted overnight as it were from *Dorf* to *Grossstadt*, from *Gemeinschaft* to *Gesellschaft*, the migrants struggled to keep their traditional values and institutions from eroding against the forces of modernity. Although migrants often first decided to migrate in order better to provide for their extended family back home, attachments inevitably weakened under the strain of long separations and far distances. Fathers strove to maintain the same patriarchal structure in the nuclear family in Germany, but soon economic necessity demanded that the wife leave the safe confines of the home to take outside employment; traditional gender roles collapsed. First-generation migrants endeavored to impart to their children the traditional family values of obedience and solidarity. But in the German schools, the children learned the opposite values of individualism and self-determination. Parents tried to force their children to speak the mother tongue, take pride in the homeland, and stay true to old religious mores, but the children preferred German, identified with Germany, and dismissed their parents' beliefs as antiquated. Everywhere challenged by rapid change, migrants sought to cling to tradition, but in vain. Ursula Neumann in an oft-cited study of Turkish families argued that this clinging to tradition

23 See Gerhard Eiselt, 'Islamischer Religionsunterricht und öffentlichen Schulen in der Bundesrepublik Deutschland,' *Die Öffentliche Verwaltung* (March 1981): 205–211.

is not to be understood as a natural continuation of the lifestyle in the homeland, rather as a defense against the changed environment. The confrontation with the divergent ways of the surrounding world creates in every case a sense of uncertainty, a strain on the personality. [This leads] to signs of retreat and compensation, such as exaggeration of traditional norms and values, idealizing the homeland, avoidance of contact with the German environment.[24]

It takes no great sophistication to realize that this is virtually the same stereotype of the prewar German that, as we saw in Chapter 2, emerged in the postwar attempts to explain the collapse of Weimar. Neumann's Turkish family is that same traditional, authoritarian family trying to stave off modern change which Adorno and others found in the Weimar Republic. The migrant's wish to preserve the old amidst the new is the same effort to maintain an outmoded culture in a modern society that Dahrendorf and so many others discerned in imperial Germany.

Predictably, studies of migrants diagnosed similar problems and pathologies to those common among prewar Germans. 'Anomie,' 'anxiety,' 'culture shock,' 'identity confusion,' 'fragmentation of the self-image,' 'deficient self-confidence,' 'deficient ego identity,' 'psychic overload,' 'socio-cultural stress,' were all disorders identified among migrants, especially in the second generation, the so-called 'lost generation' (*'verlorene Generation'*), which lived 'between two worlds.' Deviant behavior was the result: resignation, escapism, excessive consumption, aggression, crime.[25]

24 Ursula Neumann, *Erziehung ausländischer Kinder* (Düsseldorf: Pädagogischer Verlag Schwann, 1980), p. 23.
25 Three works that were influential in exposing the social and psychological problems of foreign youths are: Ursula Boos-Nünning, Manfred Hohmann, and R. Reich (eds), *Schulbildung ausländischer Kinder* (Bonn: Eichholz Verlag, 1976); Franz Ronneberger (ed.), *Türkische Kinder in Deutschland* (Nuremberg: Nürnberger Forschungsvereinigung, 1977); and Peter Alexis Albrecht and Christian Pfeiffer, *Die Kriminalisierung junger Ausländer* (Munich: Juventa-Verlag, 1979).

But the scariest symptom was political extremism. In the summer of 1977, the report of a North Rhine-Westphalian school official named Renate Irskens focused national attention on the problem of extremism. She claimed that fanatic Islamic fundamentalist organizations were rapidly gaining influence in the migrant community. They were zealously recruiting Turkish youths into their Koran schools and sports clubs where hatred, bigotry, and intolerance were taught.[26] North Rhine-Westphalia's Education Minister announced the establishment of a special commission to investigate and combat the problem (out of which eventually grew the decision to introduce Islamic instruction in the public schools). In his memorandum, Kühn alluded more than once to growing extremism and the need to counter it at school. Several other studies of Turkish extremism further publicized the problem.[27]

It was as if Irskens, Kühn, and others had a chance to correct a deadly mistake of their parents and grandparents. The Weimar elite had sat idly by in the early 1930s as the Nazis infiltrated and took control of youth organizations throughout the land. Contemporary educators were not going to repeat the mistake, even with a relatively small group of foreign youths. The fact that Turkish politics at the time – with its intense divisiveness, parliamentary paralysis, and ultimate military takeover – virtually replicated Weimar politics surely helped to jog Germans' memory and heighten their concern. Moreover, thousands of refugees from Turkey, most left- or right-wing extremists, poured into Germany, where they continued their battles in the cities' streets. A stabbing in 1981 of a leftist Turk by Islamic fundamentalists on the streets of Berlin provided graphic evidence of the gravity of the problem.

26 Her report is reprinted in *epd-Dokumentation* 35 (1977).
27 *Hintergründe türkischer extremistischer islamischer Aktivitäten in der Bundesrepublik Deutschland* (Düsseldorf: Deutscher Gewerkschatsbund, 1980); Barbara Hoffmann, Michael Opperskalski, and Erden Solmaz, *Graue Wölfe, Koranschulen, Idealistenvereine: Türkische Faschisten in der Bundesrepublik* (Cologne: Pahl-Rugenstein, 1981).

What was to be done? The West German intelligentsia knew exactly what to do, for it had been done to them. The cure was re-socialization to modern liberal democratic values. Kühn made clear that the 'focus' ('*Schwerpunkt*') of integration would be 'directed at the young generation and accordingly in the pre-school and school sector.'[28] The first generation was passed over. By virtue of their age, their values were fixed, their life chances determined. But the youngsters' destinies were still open, their minds malleable. A solid education could guarantee them a good job and secure future; secondary socialization could impart the values they needed to become good citizens.

This became the central theme of the Schmidt administration's *Integrationspolitik*. Targeting the second generation was stressed in 'The Suggestions for Further Development of a Comprehensive Conception for Policy on Foreign Employment' in 1977, again in 1979 in 'The Suggestions for "the Integration of the Second Generation"' put out by the Coordinating Committee for Foreign Workers in the Ministry of Labor, and again in the Cabinet Decree of March 19, 1980 entitled 'Further Development of Aliens Policy.' Bonn earmarked more funds for foreign pupils (DM2.5 million in 1973 to DM49.5 million in 1983),[29] financed countless conferences, publications, and large-scale research projects on the topic at universities and think-tanks like the German Youth Institute, and pressed the *Länder* (who are ultimately responsible for education) to train more teachers and develop better curricula for educating foreigners. The *Länder* followed suit. Teachers' colleges established special programs in *Ausländerpädagogik* and began producing *Diplom-Ausländerpädagogen* (certified teachers of foreigners). *Land* school systems introduced new experimental projects and curricula like the Krefeld Model in North Rhine-Westphalia.

---

28 Kühn, 'Stand und Weiterentwicklung,' in Meier-Braun, *Gastarbeiter oder Einwanderer* (Frankfurt: Ullstein, 1980), p. 38.
29 *Ausländerpolitik* (Bonn: Bundesminister für Arbeit und Sozialordnung, 1985), p. 39.

The effort was massive. As Hartmut Griese has remarked, a whole 'new profession and discipline was established.'[30]

Naturally, these many projects and models had very practical aims – assess language skills, develop classroom materials, train teachers – but underlying and informing them all was a concern for promoting liberal democratic values. 'Intercultural education' (*'interkulturelle Erziehung'*) became the watchword of the schools. Educators had to stop seeing ethnic and religious pluralism in their classrooms as a liability and approach it as a great opportunity. According to two of its proponents, intercultural education, by integrating into the curricula the various backgrounds and cultures of the pupils, 'awakens understanding for foreign cultures and traditions, dismantles prejudices and nationalisms, facilitates tolerance for the strange and different, and awakens empathy for the situation of "the other" rather than competiveness.'[31] These were the essential values of a liberal democratic polity and citizenry. Thus, the migrant 'problem' could be turned into an advantage and become an integral part of the liberal democratic socialization aspired to in the schools.

Again, the potent German memory was shaping the present. As suggested in Chapter 2, postwar Germans had come to trust deeply in education. After all, the Federal Republic itself was at root a great educational experiment. The founding vision and ultimate purpose of the republic originated in the magnanimous and monumental decision of the Allies to try to democratize an entire people through re-education. And it was precisely in the late 1960s and 1970s, we learned above, that studies concluded that the great pedagogic project was succeeding. Survey research

30 'Vorwort und Einleitung,' in *Der gläserne Fremde*, ed. Hartmut Griese (Leverkusen: Leske Verlag, 1984), p. 5.
31 Helmut Essinger and Achim Hellmich, 'Unterrichtsmaterialien und - medien für eine Interkulturelle Erziehung,' in *Ausländerkinder im Konflikt*, eds H. Essinger and A. Hellmich (Königstein: Athenaeum, 1981), p. 100.

showed that Germans socialized and schooled after the war were much more likely to have internalized liberal democratic values than the generation which came of age before 1945.[32] Modern West German democracy, indeed modern West German identity, owed its existence, in the last analysis, to the transformative power of education.

Both conscience and commonsense dictated that young foreigners be exposed to the same modern education. But it was clear, as one study jointly sponsored in 1977 by the Ministries of Education in Bonn and Düsseldorf concluded, 'that foreign families cannot perform the socialization function into the society of the Federal Republic' (the same belief held about parents from the Nazi era).[33] Successful integration depended on foreign children getting into the public schools at the youngest age possible and staying there until they received the appropriate degree. Officials were aware of the high dropout rates among foreigners, due in part to failing grades but also to parents who yanked their kids from school to avoid contact with Germans. This could not be tolerated. The Executive Committee of the SPD insisted that educational requirements (*Schulpflicht*) 'must be enforced, if necessary with sanctions against the parents.'[34]

The crusade to save the migrant also served the West German self-image. For decades – some might say centuries – the illiberal people needing to be liberalized, the Germans could now change places and become the liberalizers themselves. Since the end of the war, they had compared themselves to Westerners and always come out looking like a second-rate copy of the original. The migrants offered a

32 The findings are summarized in David Conradt, 'Changing German Political Culture,' in *The Civic Culture Revisited*, eds Gabriel Almond and Sidney Verba (Boston: Little, Brown & Company, 1980), pp. 256–258.

33 Ursula Boos-Nünning and Manfred Hohmann, 'Zusammenfassung: Zur Interpretation interkultureller Spannungsfelder,' in Boos-Nünning and Hohmann, *Ausländische Kinder*, p. 315.

34 'Leitlinien der SPD zur Ausländerpolitik, Beschluss des Parteivorstandes vom 28. Juni 1982,' in *Ausländerpolitik* (Bonn: Sozialdemokratische Partei Deutschlands, 1984), p. 8.

reference group which would reflect back a positive self-image. For surely the liberalizer was genuinely liberal, the democratizer genuinely democratic. Or so it had always seemed with the Western Allies.

Statements on and proposals for integration exuded a smug pride and self-confidence rare in other areas of German politics. Pride came with the knowledge that the German state, again faced with a large minority, would this time take a tolerant, welcoming, in short, liberal, approach to the problem. The danger of a nationalist revival was always mentioned, but great pride was taken in the fact that it had been and would be avoided. Self-confidence manifested itself in the certainty that liberal Enlightenment values could, like some grand elixir, cure migrants' problems and heal the wounds of ethnic discord. Always living with the memory of how their parents and grandparents had treated minorities, West German leaders, by assisting migrants, could feel good about themselves again. Integrationists could feel confident of their genuine liberalism. The integration of migrants thus represented a sort of final, self-confirming step in the broader integration of the West German people into the Western community.

POSTPONING POLITICS

This approach to integration had grave political consequences for foreigners. It led Social Democrats to postpone the granting of equal political rights to migrants while forging ahead with social and economic reforms. 'Postpone' is the critical term here. For Social Democrats never flatly denied equal rights of political participation to migrants. Kühn had argued that integration must ultimately absorb migrants into the political process either through naturalization or the extension of local voting rights (*kommunales Wahlrecht*) to those who did not wish to become German citizens. This was incumbent on policy-makers due to their liberal conscience, which dictated that all human beings regardless of race, gender, creed, or ethnicity should have the right to participate in decisions that affect their destiny.

But the Social Democrats put off making good on this promise. A party *communiqué* of 1982 stated their position: 'The introduction of local voting rights does not seem sensible [*sinnvoll*] at this time.'[35] No doubt they feared the fierce legal battle which would certainly ensue over the interpretation of Article 20 of the Basic Law, which reserves the right to vote to citizens. No doubt they also worried about alienating working-class Germans who would feel threatened by enfranchised migrants.

But beneath these immediate concerns lay a deeper, ubiquitous anxiety inherited from the past over the fragility of democracy. West German elites have a hard time seeing democracy as a strong form of government which *naturally* wins people's allegiance. Rather, remembering Weimar, they tend to see it as a frail thing which must constantly be defended against its enemies. The failure to do so had been the tragedy of Weimar; the success in doing so the triumph of the Federal Republic. This understanding of history also meant that German officials connected their very own *raison d'être* with protecting democracy, with carrying out the function of 'vigilant democracy.'

But in the 1970s, when the migrant problem arose, this critical self-defining and self-legitimating function started to fade. As discussed in the previous chapter, the threat of a mass anti-democratic movement, from the left or right, had all but evaporated by that time. Even when communist and neo-Nazi parties were allowed to organize and put up candidates for office, they never received even close to the 5 per cent of votes necessary to gain access to parliament. The state had to direct its anti-democratic paranoia at individual 'extremists' (Brandt's *Radikalenerlass*) or at small bands of terrorists (Schmidt's war with the Baader-Meinhof gang).

Migrants represented the only *mass* contingent of would-be extremists in the land. And they appeared that way

35 Ibid., p. 8.

because integrationists had stereotyped them as suffering from the same socio-cultural virus which bred so much extremism among Germans before the war. Moreover, as mentioned above, the migrants seemed to be organizing into many associations, some formidable. By 1980, there were allegedly more than 1,000 mosques in Germany. Most were no bigger than a single room, but most had Koran schools attached to them. Nevertheless, the world's attention was riveted on the explosive political potential of Islam exhibited in the Islamic Revolution in Iran. In Germany, the best-organized associations among migrants were Islamic fundamentalist. Cologne was headquarters to the Association of Islamic Cultural Centers, which boasted 20,000 members and control over 300 mosques. Berlin had an equally visible Islamic fundamentalist group in the Islamic Federation of Berlin. Across the way, so to speak, the exiled Communist Party of Turkey had its headquarters in East Berlin; but from there it controlled the more than 80 local chapters and 15,000 members of the Federation of Workers' Associations from Turkey in West Germany. And Turkey's two extreme nationalist parties (the National Salvation Party and the Nationalist Movement Party) had cells throughout the Federal Republic under names such as Union of Turkish Idealists or Islamic Union.[36]

So it seemed 'sensible at this time' to postpone the enfranchisement of migrants. It is telling that the very next line of the same *communiqué* read: 'The activities of anti-democratic and criminal migrant organizations are to be monitored with all available legal and organizational means.'[37] Even Kühn, an advocate of voting rights for foreigners, argued that migrant political parties should not be permitted; rather migrants would have to choose between existing German political parties. Berlin's mayor, Dietrich

36 For description and analysis of this complex and confusing mosaic of Turkish migrant associations, see the special edition of *Forum* 1 (March, April, May 1986).
37 'Leitlinien,' in *Ausländerpolitik*, p. 8.

Stobbe, perhaps best expressed the widespread anxiety when in 1979 he claimed: 'Given the current state of integration, there exists the danger that German parties would be driven out of the district assemblies and radical foreign groups voted in.'[38]

Social Democrats preferred to postpone full political rights until integration progressed further. And by this they meant until the migrants were absorbed into the key structures of West German society and until the schools had time to rear a second generation of migrants fully socialized to modern liberal democratic norms and values. In 1980, a statement from Schmidt's cabinet indicated that foreigners demonstrated their 'willingness and ability to integrate' (*'Integrationswilligkeit und -fähigkeit'*) when they 'have obtained a degree from a secondary or higher school, have completed vocational training, or have regularly attended full-time programs of professional training for one year.'[39] To have done any of these things, a foreign pupil would have most likely have had to attend German schools from a very young age.

But while the schools properly socialized young migrants, officials still felt foreigners deserved a voice in the policy-making process. At every level of government, so-called 'Foreigners' Councils' (*'Ausländerbeiräte'*) were established to advise policy-makers. Typically, prominent migrants were appointed to the councils, and in some areas members were elected in elections held among the general migrant population. The latter, in particular, were seen as a forerunner to the introduction of local voting rights as well as a testing ground to see how migrants would vote.[40]

The Social Democrats remained true to their integrative goals – and liberal conscience. Although they lost control of

38 *Frankfurter Rundschau*, March 26, 1979.
39 *Informationsbrief Ausländerrecht* (April 1980): 220.
40 See Lutz Hoffmann, *Beiräte – Wahlrecht – Bürgerrecht. Zur politischen Partizipation der nichtdeutschen Einwohner in der Bundesrepublik Deutschland* (Frankfurt: Dagyeli Verlag, 1989).

the *Bundestag* in 1982, they continued to press for improved political rights for migrants. In 1987, claiming integration had progressed far enough, the SPD came out in favor of local voting rights for foreigners. In 1989, the party called for a radical liberalization of naturalization policy, including automatic citizenship for foreign children born in Germany (with at least one parent also born there, however) and a right to citizenship for those 'who at the end of their tenth year of life have long resided here legally.' 'We are of the opinion,' said the party spokesman, 'that especially for foreigners of the second and third generation, the path to German citizenship must be opened up as other neighboring European lands have long since done.'[41]

This cautious, piecemeal approach to politically empowering migrants made perfect sense to Germans. The Allies had adopted a similar strategy after the war in returning sovereignty to the defeated foe. First appointing trusted leaders, then holding special supervised elections with certain 'dangerous' parties prohibited, leading finally to full sovereignty; the direct analogies to the foreigner advisory councils, local voting rights, and ultimately naturalization are too obvious to miss. To the foreigners, the Germans were doing what had once been done to them. Like the West Germans, the migrants would have to prove they were worthy and capable of governing themselves; and they would be tested – but also assisted – just as thoroughly as the Germans had been.

Integrationspolitik reflected a firmly rooted liberal conscience in the republic's leaders, but one with a pronounced technocratic slant to it. Liberal values were not understood as natural, rather learned. Nor were democratic rights seen as natural, or inalienable, but earned and awarded. It was for this reason that the phrase 'willingness and ability to integrate' became so commonly used to distinguish between desirable and undesirable migrants ('He who wishes to stay here must be willing to integrate. . . . He who resists should

41 *Die SPD im Deutschen Bundestag* (March 23, 1989).

realize that this can in the last result mean the loss of his residence permit'[42]). All the rhetoric to the contrary notwithstanding, integration was not a right guaranteed migrants as human beings living in Germany, but a privilege they were to earn by learning to be a certain kind of human being, a liberal human being.

42 'Leitlinien,' in *Ausländerpolitik*, p. 8.

4

CONSERVATIVE
LIBERALISM 1982–1990

We desire full legal equality for foreigners. This goal can
only be reached if foreigners are willing to apply for German
citizenship with all its rights and duties. Naturalization must
be the final outcome of the process of integration; it is also
for us the key to obtaining the right to vote.

(Resolution of the 37th Congress of the Christian Democratic
Union)

INTRODUCTION

The return of the Christian Democrats to the ruling coalition
in 1982 seemed to signal a revival of German nationalism.
Chancellor Kohl and his conservative colleagues felt the
nation hamstrung by a scarcity of national pride. For the
remainder of the decade, Germans heard an endless litany
of public calls to renew German patriotism. Polls showed
80 per cent of Americans voiced pride in being American,
whereas only 20 per cent of West Germans were proud of
being German. Low self-esteem conservatives blamed on the
nation's now fossilized hang-up with Hitler and the Holocaust. West Germans continued to saddle themselves with
the guilt and shame over the Third Reich (thus the many
public ceremonies, programs, and publications of 1983 to
commemorate the 50th anniversary of the Nazi seizure of
power). But four-fifths of the contemporary West Germans,

including the young Chancellor, came of age after 1945 and therefore bore neither direct nor indirect responsibility for Hitler's crimes. Moreover, there was much more to German history than the sordid years from 1933 to 1945. West Germans had to stop viewing their past, complained Franz Josef Strauss, 'as an endless chain of mistakes and crimes.' It was time for West Germany 'to emerge from the shadow of the Third Reich' and 'become a normal nation again.' It was time for West Germans to 'walk tall.'[1]

Kohl set out to do many things to restore patriotism. He announced plans to construct two new museums of national history and stacked the advisory commissions with conservative historians. He permitted public television networks to show Germany in its borders of 1937 when forecasting the weather. He revived the long-dormant calls to reunify Germany. And he invited Ronald Reagan to pay tribute to the German soldiers resting in Bitburg cemetery, even though some of Himmler's Waffen-SS men were buried there.

Most disturbing was his attempt to divert attention away from the Nazi years. In the plans for museums, for example, the years 1933–1945 were to appear as no more than a brief blip in a long national history. Kohl also attacked the common interpretation of the Holocaust as uniquely evil. For instance, he equated Gorbachev with Goebbels. He even tried to put a positive spin on the Nazis by claiming they worked, misguidedly no doubt, on the side of the West against communism.

These acts ignited a political firestorm, culminating in the great *Historikerstreit* (historians' debate) of 1986. For a year, the land's most prominent scholars debated back and forth in the editorial pages of the leading newspapers over whether the Final Solution was unique in human history. But the debate was about much more than the interpretation of past

1 Quoted in Richard Evans, *In Hitler's Shadow* (New York: Pantheon, 1989), p. 19.

events. As always with the Holocaust, it was about Germany's future too. Thus Habermas charged that the new attitude threatened to undermine the Germans' greatest achievement, namely, their postwar commitment to Enlightenment liberalism. Conservatives, led by historians Ernst Nolte and Michael Stürmer, rebutted with the argument that the obsession with Hitler and the Holocaust made it impossible for West Germans to develop a positive attitude about themselves or their government.[2]

Unhysterical observers eventually downplayed the revived nationalism. In his book on the historians' debate, Richard Evans concluded that the arch-conservatives were ultimately marginalized and disrespected in the academy.[3] Writing in 1987, Peter Katzenstein could detect no major shift in public policy.[4] Studies of West German political culture continued to find widespread support for modern liberal values.[5] And surely what little real change did occur now seems insignificant in the light of Unification. What was dramatically dubbed the '*Wende*' (the turn) really amounted to only a slight bend in the road. Arch-conservatives got the chance to say some things that were taboo in the 1970s but not much chance to kill the dominant liberal consensus.

Analysis of *Ausländerpolitik* during those years bears out this more tempered conclusion. Kohl's nationalist rhetoric never translated, as was feared, into much anti-migrant legislation. On the contrary, in liberalizing the requirements for naturalization in 1990 Kohl's government would open the republic's doors wider than ever for non-Germans.

But this does not mean that no *Wende* occurred. It did; only it took place within liberalism itself rather than against it. For the Christian Democrats sought to relieve the state of its responsibility of liberalizing the republic and its citizens.

2 Ernst Nolte and Michael Stürmer, *Historikerstreit* (Munich: Piper, 1987).
3 Evans, *In Hitler's Shadow*, pp. 122–123.
4 Peter Katzenstein, *Policy and Politics in West Germany* (Philadelphia: Temple University Press, 1987).
5 See Ronald Inglehart, *Culture Shift in Advanced Industrial Society* (Princeton: Princeton University Press, 1990).

This mission was done, *fait accompli*. In *Ausländerpolitik*, the government abandoned the SPD's policy of trying to force migrants to integrate and left the decision to the individual migrant. Furthermore, voluntary integration was understood, in the end, as the decision to naturalize, to become a citizen of the republic.

But like the Social Democratic approach in the 1970s, the Christian Democratic approach in the 1980s served the interests of its authors. The new tack further upgraded the self-image of West Germans and, once again, with disastrous political consequences for foreigners.

NATIONALIST RHETORIC

'The number of foreign fellow citizens must be reduced.' With this statement, made shortly before becoming Chancellor in 1982, Kohl echoed, encouraged, and exploited the anti-foreigner sentiment in public opinion that had been brewing since 1979. The great oil shock of that year, like the first one in 1973, intensified inflation, unemployment, and, above all, anxiety. Germans who felt their economic security suddenly jeopardized reacted in the same way people did in all Western countries with large migrant populations: they vented frustration through the simplistic complaint that migrants were taking 'German' jobs; and they relieved anxiety through the vain hope that their own economic troubles would somehow disappear if only the migrants would. Some 70 per cent to 80 per cent of Germans, surveys taken between 1979 and 1982 found, opposed the permanent presence of a large foreign population in the Federal Republic.[6] The Interior Ministry documented that threats and acts of violence against foreigners more than doubled from 1980

6 See infas, *Meinungen und Einstellungen zu Ausländerproblemen, Endbericht* (Bonn-Bad Godesberg: April 1982); 'Ausländer-feindlichkeit, Exodus erwuenscht,' *Der Spiegel* (May 3, 1982): 39; or 'Ein Thema von Brisanz: Ausländer, politische Asylanten,' *Aktuelle demoskopische Berichte Allensbach* (November 6, 1981): 1.

to 1981. The publication in June 1981 of the 'Heidelberg Manifesto' by fifteen professors helped to lend greater visibility and academic legitimacy to xenophobic attitudes. The signatories warned that integration, with its goal of a 'multi-cultural society,' was causing 'the mongrelization [*Überfremdung*] of our language, our culture, and our tradition.' Citizen initiatives called 'Lists Against Foreigners' ('*Listen für Ausländerstopp*') sprang up and stood candidates for election in several *Länder*. One such list received 3.8 per cent of the vote in a local election held in Kiel in May 1982.

Kohl and his followers sensed the Social Democrats' political vulnerability on this issue. In their campaign to unseat Schmidt, the conservatives underscored his inability to govern effectively. On the migrant problem, his administration could not hide the fact that it had promised and failed after the first oil shock to reduce the number of foreigners in the land. The heightened xenophobia that followed the second shock made for an irresistibly opportune atmosphere in which to spotlight the government's ineffectiveness and contrast it with swift, decisive solutions proposed by the ambitious opposition. Conservatives stepped up their rhetoric against existing *Ausländerpolitik*, and the issue became a frequent subject of debate in the *Bundestag* during the fateful year of 1982.

Conservatives sought to blame all problems associated with migration, including increased xenophobia, on Schmidt's *Ausländerpolitik*. Thus, Carl-Dieter Spranger, soon to become parliamentary Under-Secretary in the Interior Ministry, insisted that

> this mood in the population is not the expression of a nationalist arrogance or a racist ignorance among Germans, this hostility toward foreigners is rooted not in a hostile attitude toward foreigners among Germans, rather in the policy of the federal government which has brought about the causes of this mood.[7]

7 *Deutscher Bundestag* (Plenarprotokoll 9/83): 4913.

The greatest fault of the government's policy was the failure to hold down the number of foreigners from outside the EC. According to a resolution passed by the CDU/CSU parliamentary faction on January 18, 1982, the German people had good cause to fear and oppose the kind of large-scale immigration which had taken place in the 1970s. Germany could not permit itself to become a 'country of immigration' ('*Einwanderungsland*'). In the first place, the Federal Republic bore 'as a part of a divided Germany historical and constitutional responsibility for the German nation.' It had always therefore to remain open to and prepared for émigrés 'from German-speaking territory' ('*aus dem deutschsprachigen Raum*').

In the second place, Germany, as the most densely populated country in Europe, was strictly limited in its 'absorption capabilities' ('*Aufnahmemöglichkeiten*').

> With an average foreign presence of 7 per cent [of the population] – in certain areas as much as 25 per cent – the limit of burdenability ['*Belastbarkeit*'] for our state and its population, for the infrastructure as well as for the housing and job market has been reached, in concentrated areas indeed greatly exceeded.

The resolution acknowledged Bonn's obligation to welcome the 1.5 million foreigners from other EC countries who, according to Article 48 of the Treaty of Rome, enjoyed a right to freedom of movement within the community. And in making the resolution public, faction-leader Alfred Dregger observed that these foreigners were easy to integrate 'due to their common roots in European culture.' The main problem lay with the 3.2 million foreigners from non-EC countries, in particular with the 1.5 million Turks. The Federal Republic simply could not fully and permanently integrate these foreigners into the mainstream of society. Schmidt's policy was thus deemed unfair to migrants, because in promising integration, it raised expectations which could not be fulfilled. It was also irresponsible, according to Christian Democrats, because the long-term presence of a large unintegrated migrant population inevitably sharpened animosities between foreigners and West Germans.

A responsible *Ausländerpolitik* had to slow the influx and hasten the exodus of non-EC migrants. The resolution promised in place of the 'indecisiveness' and 'inactivity' of the government prompt, effective measures, such as stricter regulations governing the immigration of dependants in the homeland, expanded police powers to deport 'political extremists and convicted criminals,' and tougher requirements for asylum-seekers.[8]

Their backs to the wall, Schmidt and his cabinet felt compelled to take a tougher stance on *Ausländerpolitik*. On November 11, 1981, it was announced that the cabinet had reached 'agreement that the immigration of family members from lands which do not belong to the European Community should be stopped with ... all legal means within the framework of the Basic Law.'[9] Two weeks later, Schmidt's government decreed an 'immediate regulation' ('*Sofortregelung*') imploring all *Länder* to reduce from 18 to 16 the age at which children of foreigners could no longer legally immigrate. On January 1, 1982, a new Law to Counter Illegal Employment took effect.

But these measures could not placate conservatives. In the *Bundesrat*, which they controlled, Christian Democrats criticized the new regulations as insufficient and submitted formal requests for the government to explore harsher restrictions against immigration as well as greater incentives for emigration. Schmidt responded on July 14 with a proposal of 'Measures to Promote the Return [Home] of Foreign Workers,' which essentially amounted to shortening the time (from 24 to 6 months) returning migrants had to wait to reclaim money they had invested in pension funds while working for German firms.

8 The resolution, along with Dregger's introductory comments, is printed in 'Union legt Konzept für eine langfristige Regelung vor,' *UiD* (January 21, 1982): 11–13.
9 Quoted in Karl-Heinz Meier-Braun, *Integration oder Rückkehr?* (Mainz: Grünwald, 1988), p. 19.

Try as he might, Schmidt could not shake off the image of himself as a softy on *Ausländerpolitik* that the conservatives labored so assiduously and effectively to project. Polls taken in 1982 showed that voters had more confidence in the CDU than the SPD to find a 'solution to the migrant question.'[10]

Kohl thus owed Schmidt's ouster in part to the anti-foreigner mood in the land. Aware of this, and the forthcoming national elections, the new Chancellor made *Ausländerpolitik* one of four points of the 'Emergency Program' delineated in his inaugural address. Kohl also announced the establishment of a new '*Kommission Ausländerpolitik*' with the charge to review and overhaul existing policy. On February 24, 1983, less than two weeks before the national elections, the Commission came out with its recommendations. They were, as promised, tough (tough enough to occasion formal dissent by most non-Christian Democratic commissioners), and included: lowering from 16 to 6 the age at which children of foreigners could no longer legally immigrate; authorizing the deportation of suspected criminals before conviction; and declaring the year-long receipt of unemployment insurance a legal ground for deportation.[11]

The election gave Kohl and his coalition partners from the FDP the parliamentary majority they desired. This they used in November to pass their own 'Law to Promote the Willingness of Foreigners to Return Home' ('*Gesetz zur Förderung der Rückkehrbereitschaft von Ausländern*'). The law went further than Schmidt's proposal by enabling returning migrants immediately to reclaim marks they had invested in pension funds. It also offered DM10,500 to each unemployed foreigner who agreed permanently to leave Germany with his or her entire family. Labeled a 'get-lost premium' by critics, the official 'return aid' ('*Rückkehrhilfe*') did seem to motivate

10 *Zwischen Toleranz und Besorgtheit, Einstellungen der deutschen Bevölkerung zu aktuellen Problemen der Ausländerpolitik* (Allensbach am Bodensee: Institut für Demoskopie Allensbach, 1985), p. 1.

11 The recommendations are reprinted in *Bericht zur Ausländerpolitik* (Bonn: Der Beauftragte der Bundesregierung für Ausländerfragen, 1984), pp. 25–32.

larger numbers of migrants to return home. In 1984, 546,457 migrants (compared to 425,189 in 1983) left, and the overall number of foreigners in Germany fell from 4.5 to 4.1 million.[12]

Such policies and proposals appeared to manifest revived nationalism. Indeed, some prominent conservatives tried to rationalize their policies as a legitimate defense of *das Volk* in openly volkish terms. Interior Minister Friedrich Zimmermann, for example, said it was understandable that many West Germans feared becoming a minority in their own land.[13] Like the *Konsolidierungspolitik* following the first oil shock, the *Rückkehrpolitik* following the second was based on the notion of putting *German* national interests first. Once again, important liberal principles guaranteed to all by the Basic Law (such as due process or the protection of the family) were to be denied to non-Germans. Kohl's plan, however, met with the same fate as that of his Social Democratic predecessors: it was never fully implemented and it ultimately failed.

ENTRENCHED LIBERALISM

The obstacles to *Rückkehrpolitik* were similar to those which had blocked *Konsolidierungspolitik* a decade earlier. The migrants refused to cooperate. Only 16,833 of them actually cashed in on the DM10,500 premium, approximately 140,000 on the immediate repayment of the pension fund. After all, the offer was limited to an eight-month period between November 1983 and June 1984. Subsequent analyses (including one conducted by the Federal Labor Institute) have cast doubt on the alleged effectiveness of the law. At best, the financial incentives enticed foreigners already planning to emigrate to leave sooner, but they failed to persuade those

---

12 See *Daten und Fakten zur Ausländersituation* (Bonn: Der Beauftragte der Bundesregierung für die Integration der ausländischen Arbeitnehmer und ihrer Familienangehörigen, 1989), p. 14.
13 Quoted in Lothar Elsner and Joachim Lehmann, *Ausländische Arbeiter unter dem deutschen Imperialismus* (Berlin: Dietz Verlag, 1988), p. 276.

who wished to stay to reverse their plans. And even this is questionable given the fact that in a number of previous years (1975, 1974) more migrants had returned home without the incentives than did in 1983.[14] It seems migrants had their own reasons for coming and going which government could not easily influence. Aware of its limited impact, Kohl's government chose not to extend the offer after June 30, 1984. In 1985, the number of returnees dropped to 366,706, and the number of foreigners in the land rose to 4.4 million; by 1987, the number was roughly the same as it was when Kohl took office (4.6 million).[15]

Sheer demographics foiled *Rückkehrpolitik* as well. Population studies conducted by governmental agencies revealed that the West German population was aging and shrinking due to greater longevity and lower birthrates. Projections predicted that the size of the West German population would fall from 60 to 55 million by the year 2000 and to 43 million by 2030. Moreover, it was estimated that in 2030, 37 per cent of West Germans would be 60 or older. Migrants showed a much different profile. Only 2.2 per cent (in 1987) were over 64, while 79.8 per cent were under 44 and 23.5 per cent under 15. In addition, the birthrates among foreign women were much higher than among West German women (twice as high among Turks). The conclusions to be drawn were crystal clear: West Germany, barring radical changes in the labor market, would become more, not less, dependent on foreign workers in the future.[16] In the long run, then, an aggressive *Rückkehrpolitik* would undermine rather than

14 Klara Osiander and Johannes Zerger, *Rückkehr in die Fremde* (Augsburg: MaroVerlag, 1988), pp. 38–42.
15 A thorough statistical profile of the migrant population can be found in *Daten und Fakten zur Ausländersituation* (Bonn: Der Beauftragte der Bundesregierung für die Integration der ausländischen Arbeitnehmer und ihrer Familienangehörigen, May 1989).
16 See *Wachsender Bedarf an ausländischen Jugendlichen* (Bonn: Der Beauftragte der Bundesregierung für die Integration der ausländischen Arbeitnehmer und ihrer Familienangehörigen, 1987); or Statistisches Bundesamt (ed.), *Datenreport 1989* (Bonn: Bundeszentrale für politische Bildung, 1989), pp. 47ff.

serve the nation's economic interests – something the influential employers' associations repeatedly stressed, just as
they had ten years before in response to *Konsolidierungspolitik*.[17] Indeed, the CDU itself had taken this same position
as far back as 1977.[18]

Kohl also faced considerable international constraints. He
too had to recognize the bilateral treaty with Turkey from
1972 in which the Federal Republic agreed that no law-
abiding Turks would be forced to return home. And as a
result of the Treaty of Association negotiated between the
EEC and Turkey in 1980, the rights of Turkish resident aliens
(for example, of receiving residence visas or protection
against deportation) became nearly identical to those of
resident aliens from the EEC.[19] In 1985, the European Commission indirectly criticized Kohl's policy by warning against
the vast problems of reintegration second-generation migrants encountered when returning home. The Commission
recommended that foreign youths be granted a right to
return to the hostland if reintegration proved too difficult.[20]

Domestic opposition also discouraged Kohl. Naturally,
migrants and their German advocates vociferously challenged the new administration's stated objectives. Thus, the
Catholic Church derogated the proposals of Kohl's special
commission as 'expulsion politics,' while the migrant association Foreign Fellow Citizens in Hesse denounced them as
a 'shocking inhumanity' and 'an absolute low point in . . .
West Germany's postwar history.' Such opposition could
not be easily ignored. In 1981 in Berlin, such groups took
to the streets in mass demonstrations against the hated
'Lummer Decree,' which made it more difficult for migrant

17 See Meier-Braun, *Integration oder Rückkehr?*, p. 73.
18 'Ausländische Arbeitnehmer – unsere Mitbürger,' *UiD Dokumentation*
(August 11, 1977): 3.
19 See Beauftragte der Bundesregierung für die Belange der Ausländer,
Bericht über die Lage der Ausländer in der Bundesrepublik Deutschland 1993
(Bonn: Beauftragte der Bundesregierung für die Belange der Ausländer,
1994), pp. 83–84.
20 See Meier-Braun, *Integration oder Rückkehr?*, p. 54.

families to reunite. Eventually, the conservative administration was forced to rescind the decree. After the 'refugee crisis' of 1986, in which for weeks during the summer East German authorities permitted thousands of refugees to stream into West Berlin via East Berlin, the CDU sought to tighten the land's laws governing political asylum; however, the party could not drum up the two-thirds support in parliament necessary to amend Article 16 of the constitution, which guarantees political asylum to all politically persecuted persons. Nevertheless, the most significant opposition to a more restrictive *Ausländerpolitik* came from within the ruling coalition itself, from the Free Democrats. True to their epithet, the 'Liberals' staunchly defended the liberal rights guaranteed foreigners in the constitution and other statutes. It did not hurt their cause that one of their own, Liselotte Funcke, was the Commissioner for Aliens. Moreover, the influential Hans-Dietrich Genscher personally intervened on more than one occasion to support Funcke in her ultimately successful efforts to block harsh measures proposed by the Christian Socialist Interior Minister Zimmermann.[21]

There were even opponents inside the Chancellor's own party. Moderates grouped around Party Secretary Heiner Geissler complained from the moment the Chancellor took office that greatly reducing the number of foreigners in the land was simply not a real option for the new government. At a special conference on 'Foreigners in Germany,' sponsored by the party in October 1982, legal experts systematically presented the 'legal limitations' to a policy of large-scale repatriation. The overwhelming majority of foreigners residing in the Federal Republic were protected against involuntary repatriation by international treaties to which Bonn was party. Moreover, measures designed to deport foreigners not protected under such treaties would likely

---

21 For a detailed discussion of the policies proposed by the Commission as well as the opposition they engendered, see Meier-Braun, *Integration oder Rückkehr?*, pp. 29–54.

violate Article 2 of the Basic Law, while measures designed to hinder or prevent family reunifications would founder on Article 6.[22] And indeed, the experts were right. In 1988, the Federal Constitutional Court struck down statutes in Bavaria and Baden-Württemberg which lengthened from one to three years the period foreigners had to wait to join their spouses living in Germany.

Well aware of the formidable legal, political, and economic obstacles to *Rückkehrpolitik*, Kohl's administration chose not to put much muscle behind the tough-sounding rhetoric of the campaign trail. In fact, none of the recommendations of the commission was made law. Once they served their function of attracting voters, they were discreetly tabled in cabinet and coalition meetings.

This is not to say that a harsh, nationalistic *Ausländerpolitik* lost all support after the election. Zimmermann and other arch-conservatives continued to try to drum up support for harsh measures until 1986, but without success.[23] In 1988, the xenophobic Republican Party burst onto the political stage by winning over 7 per cent of the vote in Berlin. But the Republicans owed their initial popularity, at least in part, to Kohl's toothless policy. For many of the original organizers and supporters of the Republican Party deserted the CDU or CSU precisely because Kohl's government refused to take the draconian steps they desired to trim back the number of foreigners.

In terms of actual policy, then, the much-touted and feared *Rückkehrpolitik* amounted to little more than paying several thousand migrants several thousand marks to leave the country. This seems tame when contrasted with the *Konsolidierungspolitik* of a decade earlier which included such real, not merely proposed, policies as the banning of foreigners from specified neighborhoods. *Rückkehrpolitik* was more rhetoric than reality.

22 See especially Gert Hammer, 'Handlungsspielraum deutscher Ausländerpolitik,' in *Ausländer in Deutschland*, ed. Heiner Geissler (Munich: Günter Olzog, 1982), pp. 148–155.
23 See Meier-Braun, *Integration oder Rückkehr?*, p. 56.

CONTINUED INTEGRATION

In many respects, Kohl's actual policy differed little from Schmidt's. Officially, the Kohl administration committed itself to the same three 'basic aims' stipulated by the Schmidt government in February 1982:

1 'to limit effectively further migration of foreigners into the Federal Republic of Germany';
2 'to promote the willingness of migrants to return home'; and
3 'to improve the economic and social integration and clarify the residency rights of those foreigners who have lived in the Federal Republic of Germany for many years.'[24]

In other words, the new administration projected the same illusion that Germany 'was not a country of immigration' and could therefore neither encourage nor normalize the permanent presence of migrants. Nevertheless, those foreigners who resided in West Germany had to be offered the same basic opportunities (*Chancengleichheit*) enjoyed by Germans.

And just like its predecessor a decade earlier, Kohl's administration did not abandon integrative programs once it became undeniable that the number of foreigners in the land could not be reduced. Shortly after the *Wende*, Zimmermann of all people formally declared integration 'an important goal' of the new administration. And his definition of integration was virtually identical to that of his predecessors, with a resolute rejection of both marginalization and assimilation and a strong emphasis on creating equal opportunity through education.

Integration does not mean the loss of one's own cultural identity. But it requires that foreigners make an effort to master the German language, respect our basic

24 *Politik Informationen aus Bonn v. Februar 1982* (Bonn: Presse- und Informationsamt der Bundesregierung, 1982).

laws and adapt enough to the relations here that a harmonious co-existence is possible. To this I add that children of foreign workers should enter the Federal Republic early enough that they can go through our school system, learn the German language, obtain a degree and thereby a chance to acquire an apprentice-ship or job. If this opportunity for integration is not taken advantage of, the emergence of a marginal social group without future opportunities is preordained.[25]

Nor was this mainly rhetoric like *Rückkehrpolitik*. The conservatives devoted considerable resources and energies to integration throughout the 1980s. Federal funding for integration was not cut back, rather expanded (albeit incre-mentally).[26] Old programs were continued and many new ones started.[27] And basic social indicators suggested slow but steady progress in the level of integration. Taken as a kind of statistical conglomerate, migrants had slightly better residency and working rights in the 1980s than in the 1970s; they made a little more money; they lived in somewhat roomier and cleaner apartments; they spoke better German and had more German friends; and their children were more likely to obtain a degree and gainful employment.[28]

This is not to say integration succeeded brilliantly during the 1980s. It should be noted (as it was forcibly by Funcke in a study published shortly before she tendered her

25 Bundesminister des Innern (ed.), *Ausländerpolitik* (Bonn: Bonner Universitäts-Buchdruckerei, 1983), p. 3.
26 See Bundesminister für Arbeit und Sozialordnung (ed.), *Ausländerpolitik* (Bonn: Bundersminister für Arbeit und Sozialordnung, 1985).
27 For a summary of all programs for foreigners, see *Orientierungshilfen für Ausländer* (Bonn: Beauftragte der Bundesregierung für die Integration der ausländischen Arbeitnehmer und Ihrer Familienangehörigen, 1986); for a summary of new initiatives, see Wolfgang Ohndorf, 'Ausländer-integration: neue Massnahmen,' *Bundesarbeitsblatt* (January 3, 1991): 5–9.
28 For a detailed summary of 'Repräsentativuntersuchung '85,' the government-commissioned evaluation of the level of integration de-signed to parallel similar studies commissioned in 1968, 1972, and 1980, see Peter Fendrich, 'Integration Kommt voran,' *Bundesarbeitsblatt* (December 1986): 9–12.

resignation in 1991) that in practically every category of integration, migrants continued to lag far behind the average German in terms of rights, privileges, and opportunities.[29] So it would be misleading to maintain that integration received a great boost in the 1980s. But it would be equally misleading to insinuate, like so many critics of the Kohl administration,[30] that integration dissipated or even attenuated after the *Wende*. It grew laggardly as if by accretion.

LIBERALISM REDEFINED

We would be similarly misled if we accepted charges that conservative *Ausländerpolitik* was disingenuous. More punctilious critics confess that the Kohl administration did not actually go through with the severe measures hectored about shortly before and after the *Wende*. However, these critics attribute official timidity, often in self-congratulatory fashion, to effective opposition from the left. Had progressives not made a stink, they aver, Christian Democrats would have realized their racist objectives.[31] Relentless suspicion of thinly veiled anti-democratic motives and maneuvers among conservative politicians has become endemic to the German left since the collapse of the Weimar Republic. As regards *Ausländerpolitik*, such cynicism has indeed played an important part in exposing or discouraging genuinely racist personalities or proposals in government. But it also can blind us to the efforts of many influential conservatives within the CDU who favored and fought for a more flexible and

---

29 *Bericht der Beauftragten der Bundesregierung für die Integration der ausländischen Arbeitnehmer und Ihrer Familienangehörigen* (Bonn: Beuftragte der Bundesregierung für die Integration der ausländischen Arbeitnehmer und Ihrer Familienangehörigen, 1991).

30 See, for example, Elsner and Lehmann, *Ausländische Arbeiter*, pp. 271ff.

31 See, for example, Stephen Castles, 'The Guests Who Stayed – The Debate on "Foreigners' Policy" in the German Federal Republic,' *International Migration Review* 19 (Fall 1985): 530–532.

generous policy toward migrants.[32] This is regrettable not so much because many pro-migrant 'heroes' go unsung; but because it was precisely these moderates or liberal conservatives who effected a subtle but significant shift in the way the federal government conceptualized, exercised, and legitimized *Ausländerpolitik*. More importantly, the shift represented a further step in the direction of liberalism, not a retreat backward toward erstwhile nationalism.

Liberal conservatives contested a more restrictive *Ausländerpolitik* for *moral* as well as practical reasons. As noted, they deemed the Commission's proposals unimplementable. But many also adjudged them incompatible with the party's Christian ethic. At the aforementioned party conference on migration held in 1982, Marlies Schieren opened her address by quoting St Paul's injunction to the Romans (14:10) that: 'You should never pass judgement on a brother or treat him with contempt.'[33] Nor was Schieren's the lone voice of a zealot tolerated but ignored by the impious crowd. Later at the CDU's 37th Party Congress in 1989, which included a major debate over *Ausländerpolitik*, both Norbert Blum and Heiner Geissler, hardly backbenchers, reminded their colleagues that the party's position should accord with the Christian precept of respecting the worth and dignity of each individual, regardless of race or nationality. Christian Democrats had, in other words, a religious obligation to create a 'climate friendly to foreigners in our land' (to quote from the formal resolution drawn up at the end of the Congress).[34]

Others keen to make their party conscientious invoked the venerable tradition of the German *Aufklärung*. Party func-

---

32 Generally speaking, this group or wing of the party was led by Labor Minister Norbert Blum and party General Secretary Heiner Geissler. Their chief supporters were located in the party's Social Committee, the Christian Democratic Workers' Union (CDA), and the offices of Christian Democratic Commissioners for Foreigners in the *Länder*.

33 Marlies Schieren, 'Urteile und Vorurteile – Meinungen und Einstellungen,' in Geissler, *Ausländer in Deutschland*, p. 137.

34 *37. Bundesparteitag der Christlich Demokratischen Union Deutschlands: Niederschrift* (Bonn: Union Betrieb-GmbH, 1989), pp. 378–379, 470.

tionary Warnfried Dettling, for example, with secular, but no less righteous, resolve, enjoined members to honor Kant's categorical imperative and seek to approximate his noble vision of a republic open to all humans. And using foreigners as 'scapegoats' or forcing them to exit the republic, he maintained, scarcely seemed in keeping with the enlightened morality of such great thinkers as Goethe, Schiller, and Kant.[35]

But the loudest liberal voices came from fervent *Verfassungspatrioten*. These defenders of the constitution underscored the constitutional obligation the CDU now had as a ruling party to adopt and administer a liberal, tolerant, humane *Ausländerpolitik*. Moreover, they did not neglect but did look beyond the letter to the spirit of the law. The Basic Law had been conceived in the hope of creating a free, democratic society open to and protective of diverse and different persons, opinions, and lifestyles – a society in which the Nuremberg Laws, *Krystallnacht*, or Auschwitz were impossible, nay unthinkable. And although West Germany had no ethnic minorities to speak of at its inception, it was argued, it had, like all the other major industrial nations, developed since then into a *de facto* country of immigration with the accompanying ethnic pluralism. A 'free democracy' had to promote tolerance for 'diversity' as well as appreciation for the 'enrichment' it brings. 'The Federal Republic,' Geissler claimed, 'stood before a great challenge in the next year and decades' – the challenge to realize the essence of the constitution (that is, 'the inviolable worth of each individual') not only for Germans but for the non-German minority now living permanently amongst them. If the West Germans could meet 'the great demands' of this challenge, he added, they would pass yet another 'test' as the 'democratic and social federal state' prescribed in Article 20.[36] This idea – that *Ausländerpolitik* was more than a peripheral issue

35 Warnfried Dettling, 'Identitätskrise oder: Die Angst vor dem Fremden,' in Geissler, *Ausländer in Deutschland*, pp. 11–13.
36 Geissler's remarks are quoted in Schieren, 'Urteile,' p. 144.

but somehow a central and defining mission for the West German people – reverberated through the moderate circles of the party. In this vein, a report commissioned in the early 1980s by the Berlin Senate (which was dominated by the CDU) concluded with great earnestness that our 'policy in the end reflects the democratic and social quality of our commonwealth.'[37]

No one trumpeted this liberal message more eloquently or cogently than Dieter Oberndörfer. In newspapers, journals, and speeches the Christian Democratic university professor launched a personal crusade to prevail upon his compatriots that their polity was first a federal republic and only second a German nation-state. His argument had extraordinary force because he cleverly and clearly juxtaposed liberal republicanism against volkish nationalism. The latter determined citizenship through the ultimately 'racist' idea of organic ethnic solidarity and pure lineage ('right blood') and had been Germany's *raison d'être* in the Second Reich, its disgrace and disaster in the Third. Republicanism, by contrast, was based on universal rather than particularistic values. It, like the opening articles of the Basic Law, placed highest worth on the individual and defined the state's mission as the protection of the individual's natural rights regardless of race, religion, nationality, etc. Theoretically at least, citizenship in a republic had to be open to all human beings.

If nationalism had been the prevailing ideology of the nineteenth century, republicanism was destined to be so for the twentieth and twenty-first. Irreversible global interdependence, Oberndörfer stressed, made the ideal of an ethnically pure polity atavistic. Already, classic republics like France and the United States, which granted citizenship on the basis of *jus soli*, were well on their way to becoming truly multi-ethnic polities with no predominant ethnic group. West Germany, however, still adhered to the

37 Ibid., p. 146.

92

anachronistic principle of *jus sanguinis* in that Article 116 of the constitution reserved the status of citizen to ethnic Germans. There existed therefore an uncomfortable 'tension' in the Federal Republic 'between the ethnic nationalist tradition and universal republican values.' With a shrewd turn of argument, Oberndörfer insisted that Article 116 was actually unconstitutional itself because it violated the proscription against ethnic discrimination in the more fundamental Article 3. 'In the multi-ethnic society of the future,' he concluded, 'only constitutional patriotism and not relics from the ideological attic of the nineteenth century can form the legitimate foundation of our commonwealth.' And this necessitated first and foremost a radical liberalization of naturalization policy so that immigrants – especially their children – could easily become citizens.[38]

If Geissler was the most visible, Oberndörfer the most cerebral partisan of the pro-migrant camp, Barbara John was the most pragmatic. The popular Commissioner for Aliens for the city of Berlin had a special gift for pointing out the absurd, but still real consequences of her country's anomalous naturalization policy. At the party congress in 1989, for instance, she reported that while roughly 54,000 aliens were born in Germany annually, only 14,000 foreigners became German citizens each year (the lowest rate in the industrial world). And although these often third-generation youngsters would likely live their entire lives in West Germany, learn to speak German better than their 'mother tongue,' and visit their 'homelands' for holidays only, the majority of them would remain 'foreigners' in the eyes of the law. If these lopsided trends were allowed to continue, she exclaimed, 'we will be speaking of foreigners of the 25th generation before too long. That is a contradiction of terms.' For John, the party had no alternative but to pursue a

38 Dieter Oberndörfer, 'Der Nationalstaat – ein Hindernis für das dauerhafte Zusammenleben mit ethnischen Minderheiten?,' *Zeitschrift für Ausländerrecht und -politik* 1 (1989): 3–13.

'generous and offensive policy of naturalization' ('*Einbürger-ungspolitik*').[39]

These liberal voices did not go unheeded. Throughout the 1980s, various proposals for a more liberal immigration policy were shuffled back and forth between ministries. By the time the Chancellor gave his second inaugural address on March 18, 1987, one could already detect a more conciliatory tone. He referred to the cultural 'enrichment' ('*Bereicherung*') won through interaction with foreigners and announced his administration's intention 'to create greater legal security [for foreigners] by amending the Aliens Law.' Following suit, the party formally resolved in 1989 significantly to liberalize the requirements for naturalization.[40] A few months later, the administration proposed and the *Bundestag* passed an entirely new Aliens Law to replace the one of 1965. The especially difficult and particularly nationalistic requirements for citizenship (adequate housing, expensive fees, proven knowledge of German language and customs) were abolished. Instead, aliens under the age of 23 were granted a right (*Anspruch*) to naturalize so long as they had resided in Germany at least eight years, had attended school there for six, and had not been convicted of a felony (Paragraph 85). Those 23 and older had to have lived in Germany for at least fifteen years, not have been convicted of a felony, and not be collecting social assistance (Paragraph 86).

Although upstaged by the drama of Unification, the new law represented a major advancement toward liberalism – ironically at the same time the Germans finally achieved national unity. Despite its commitment to integration, the SPD never deviated as a ruling party from the legal interpretation of the Supreme Administrative Court, whereby naturalization was termed 'an exception that comes into consideration only in individual cases in which it seems to

39 37. *Bundesparteitag*, p. 374.
40 Ibid., pp. 470–473.

be in the interest of the State.'[41] The new law normalized the naturalization of immigrants. Foreigners born in West Germany (roughly 1 million) would now be able to obtain German citizenship as the rule rather than the exception. Granted, the new law did not go so far as to abolish Article 116. In fact, its significance grew leaps and bounds once ethnic Germans from Eastern Europe were free to emigrate. And it cannot be denied that much more relaxed requirements for citizenship (most notably, dual citizenship) are imaginable, indeed desirable, from a liberal perspective. All the same, the Aliens Law of 1990 put the new Germany on course for evolving a multi-ethnic citizenry made up not only of native Germans, but also of Spanish, Greek, Turkish, and other Germans much like the Irish, Mexican, African, and other Americans in the classic immigration country and liberal republic across the Atlantic. 'Greek German,' 'Turkish German'; the appellations still have an awkward, even incredible, ring to them – all the more reason to acknowledge the magnitude of this conceptual shift in how liberal Christian Democrats wanted to understand their polity and people.

Christian Democrats agreed on a liberal policy, however, for political as well as moral reasons. Like the SPD's *Integrationspolitik*, the CDU's *Einbürgerungspolitik* fortified the party's broader political project. In the first place, it enabled Christian Democrats not only to dodge criticisms from the left, but also to score some against their opponents. The volkish *Rückkehrpolitik* may have generated votes for the CDU among the West German masses, but, as noted above, it laid the party open to incriminating charges of revived nationalism and racism from the progressive elite – always an uncomfortable political position in which to be in the post-Hitler era. By contrast, Christian Democrats could and

41 Quoted in William Rogers Brubaker, 'Citizenship and Naturalization: Policies and Politics,' in *Immigration and the Politics of Citizenship in Europe and North America*, ed. W.R. Brubaker (Lanham: University Press of America, 1989), p. 111.

did boast of a liberal *Einbürgerungspolitik* fairer and more progressive than anything enacted or entertained by the opposition.

Only 'German citizenship with all its rights and duties,' the party platform declared, could guarantee 'full legal equality for foreigners.' Proposals advanced by the Social Democrats and Greens which enabled and encouraged migrants to remain legal aliens indefinitely were assailed as inadequate and insidious. Thus, the party rejected Social Democratic initiatives to grant foreigners the right to vote in local elections on the grounds that they perpetuated inequality and exploitation. Most of the issues that directly affected and interested migrants (immigration law, social welfare, foreign policy) were made at the federal and *Land* level. Restricting foreigners' voice to the localities would therefore do nothing more than create the illusion of political empowerment – a kind of 'sham suffrage' (*'Scheinmitbestimmung'*).[42] Worse, the proposals gave the objectionable impression that (a) the act of voting at the local level was somehow less important and (b) foreigners were somehow less worthy of equal political rights. To Norbert Blum, the plans sounded alarmingly similar to the notorious 'three-class franchise' (*'Dreiklassenwahlrecht'*) used in Prussia during the Second Empire to perpetuate *Junker* hegemony.[43]

If red proposals were too tight with political rights, the green ones were too loose. In 1984, the Greens introduced legislation in the *Bundestag* which sought to grant aliens a 'right to settle' (*'Niederlassungsrecht'*) after five years of legal residency. According to this bill, foreigners would after that time enjoy all the rights of citizenship (including suffrage and freedom from extradition) without formally having to become West German citizens. Christian Democrats attacked and eventually defeated the proposal with the curious

42 Johannes Gerster, 'Kommunales Wahlrecht für Ausländer verzögert die Integration,' *CDU/CSU Fraktion im Deutschen Bundestag Pressedienst* (July 21, 1987).

43 *37. Bundesparteitag*, p. 368.

argument that it would inflame ethnic tensions. Conferring all the privileges of citizenship on migrants while exempting them from all its duties (particularly military service) was akin to having a permanent houseguest who was not expected to chip in with the chores. With time, the host becomes resentful; so too would the West German people. Hence, despite its apparent magnanimity, a right to settle would wind up 'giving a boost to right-wing extremism among our people.'[44] Moreover, migrants would have to live in constant fear that as mere legislation, their 'right' to settle could be rescinded at any time by a simple parliamentary majority. The rights of citizenship, however, were anchored in the constitution and permanently protected from infringement. In the last analysis, proposals from the left side of the aisle all treated foreigners as 'second-class citizens' of one sort or the other. Was the issue really so hard to resolve, asked Christian Democrats? If one wanted to make migrants fully equal to West German citizens, why not simply make them West German citizens? Perhaps it was those on the left who had the inveterate aversion to disassociating German citizenship from *das Volk*.[45]

The CDU declared its policy superior on the basis that it alone respected the migrants' right freely to choose their destiny. Proposals from the left imperiously assigned foreigners rights and status without ever giving them the opportunity to decide whether they wanted them or not. A truly liberal democratic state had to protect the individual's free choice. This emphasis on migrants' right to choose became the hallmark of the CDU's policy and accordingly turned up in practically every party statement on immigration.[46] Kohl himself let it be known in his first inaugural

---

44 Ibid., p. 376.
45 These criticisms are best articulated in Barbara John, 'Ausländerpolitik für Inländer?,' *Zeitschrift für Ausländerrecht und Ausländerpolitik* 1 (1985): 5–7.
46 See, for instance, the recapitulation of the CDU's 'concept for *Ausländerpolitik*' in *Bericht zur Ausländerpolitik*, p. 39.

address that free choice would be the kernel of his administration's *Ausländerpolitik*: 'Foreigners in Germany should be able freely to decide, but they must decide, whether they wish to return home or remain with us and integrate.' The Chancellor's remark may sound like little more than infantile chauvinism – 'My country! Love it or leave it!' In fact, it reflected a deeper commitment within his party to redefining the mission of a liberal democratic state.

At heart, Christian Democrats wanted to get the state out of the business of meddling with minds. In their eyes, government had no right to determine things as meaningful and personal as the collectivity with which one decided to identify, or the values by which one wished to live. And naturalization and integration entailed just this.

As noted, the CDU did not tamper with the definition of integration developed during the Schmidt years. For it too, integration could have nothing to do with ethnic assimilation. For each person had a right 'to live by his own cultural and religious orientations.'[47] Instead, integration entailed resocialization from the traditional norms and values of the homeland to the modern liberal ones of West Germany. And although this change might involve such mundane things as acclimatizing to the faster pace of life in industrial society, it ultimately meant internalizing a respect for 'the human dignity and moral substance of our constitution' (*'Menschenwürde und Wertordnung unserer Verfassung'*).[48] Seeing integration, like the SPD, essentially as a pedagogical process, the CDU too underscored the pivotal role the nation's schools could play in inculcating modern values among migrant pupils. The CDU did, however, add one slightly new twist to the understanding of integration. Christian Democrats insisted that naturalization was the logical outcome and best test of successful integration. In the end, only voluntary decision by a mature, rational adult to

47 37. *Bundesparteitag*, p. 471.
48 Ibid.

naturalize – to desire, appreciate, and protect the privileges and duties of democratic citizenship – could unequivocally demonstrate a person's 'ability and willingness to integrate.' Only naturalization could distinguish between what Christian Democrats called real 'inner identification' and mere instrumental 'outer identification' with the republic's core values.[49]

Precisely because integration was so personal and intimate, the state had no right to force it on individuals. In the first place, forcing change was considered futile for the age-old reason that government could not legislate morality. In the words of Commissioner John, 'integration by compulsion leads only to superficial change. . . . Processes of integration can only take place on the basis of extensive voluntarism.'[50]

More importantly, state compulsion was injurious and insensitive. Social Democrats had always recognized the significant challenge integration posed for migrants, but invariably viewed the resulting change as purely beneficial and desirable. Christian Democrats criticized this perspective as presumptuous and drew attention to the 'great sacrifices' many migrants experience in the change from traditional to modern lifestyles. They characterized integration as a 'long and difficult process' rather than a necessary or inevitable one. They went on to assemble an impressive list of reasons why migrants might wish to resist or avoid integration. Most migrants (three-quarters according to party polls) still expressed a desire to return to and reside in their homelands where traditional norms and values predominated. Even in West Germany, many migrants preferred to live in 'ethnic enclaves' in which the traditional religious, social, and cultural ways of the homeland were still honored

49 Definitions of integration can be found in II, 1 of the New Aliens Law as well as in 37. *Bundesparteitag*, Bundesminister für Arbeit, *Ausländerpolitik*, and Bundesminister des Innern, *Ausländerpolitik*.

50 Die Ausländerbeauftragte des Senats, ed., *Miteinander leben* (Berlin: Senator für Gesundheit und Soziales, 1986), p. 57.

and preserved. Was it so unnatural for a Turkish mother to want her daughter to emulate her, even if it did mean perpetuating sexist roles for women common in Turkey? Was it so unthinkable for a Greek father to want to raise his son with the same respect for elders and authority he had learned from his own father back in Greece? The individualistic, permissive, secular lifestyle of modern industrial society had become second nature to West Germans. But this did not change the fact that to many migrants it was threatening and undesirable.

In other words, Christian Democrats used the same common stereotype of migrants as people frightened by modernization. And culture shock, anomie, deprivation, schizophrenia, social frustration, criminality, aggressiveness, confusion, despair, etc., were all symptoms of 'living in the combat zone [*Spannungsfeld*] between two cultures.'[51] Christian Democrats differed from their rivals in their willingness to accept resistance to modernization as a reasonable cure for the social ills afflicting migrants. This in no way meant, however, that they themselves preferred this cure. Nor was that the point. For government in their eyes had no right to prescribe one or the other. Its role was to assist the migrant in pursuing whatever kind of treatment he himself deemed most advisable and desirable. But ultimately it was 'primarily the business of foreigners to take their destiny in Germany into their own hands and do whatever is suitable for them.'[52]

It was with this goal of minimizing the state's influence over the individual that the CDU counterbalanced the programs of integration with 'reintegration' ('*Reintegration*'). As noted already, the CDU did not reduce the resources or programs devoted to integration once it took power from the SPD. But it did feel that the state should not help just those migrants who wanted to acculturate to the modern liberal

51 *37. Bundesparteitag,* p. 471.
52 Die Ausländerbeauftragte, *Miteinander leben,* p. 59.

values dominant in West Germany. Those who wanted to resist change and preserve their traditional values while in Germany so as to be able easily to 'reintegrate' into the lifestyles of the homeland deserved equal treatment. Christian Democrats thus devoted considerable rhetorical and monetary resources to programs under the rubric 'reintegration.' These ranged from things such as supporting private migrant enterprises which tailored to special religious or ethnic needs (say, Islamic butchers) to supporting special cultural and religious organizations in the education of migrant children along very traditional lines. Some of the latter often involved granting state support to programs that were clearly based on values that contradicted those of the liberal West German conscience and constitution (most notably, Islamic instruction in Koran schools or highly nationalistic curricula and materials from the Turkish government). But Christian Democrats justified such support by arguing that the state had a duty to protect the migrants' right to choose, even if that choice was anathema to the state. The state was there to serve people, not shape them. Moreover, was this not the ultimate test of the liberal person and government: namely, the willingness to tolerate, even support, persons with views different and opposed to your own?

LIBERAL INCLUSION AND EXCLUSION

This attitude and approach, with its emphasis on free choice, hardly amount to technocratic liberalism. But the story does not end there. For, in reality, the CDU jettisoned only half of the two-pronged logic of technocratic liberalism. According to that logic, the state not only has a responsibility to mold persons into liberals, it also has the self-appointed prerogative to restrict or eliminate the political rights of suspected illiberals. The Kohl administration did not strip itself of this enormously consequential prerogative. On the contrary, Christian Democrats exacted a high political price for the luxury of free choice. Migrants who chose reintegration over integration, their homeland's passport over the Federal Republic's, had to forfeit political rights. Whereas Social Democrats had postponed political rights (until integration was complete), Christian Democrats flatly and permanently denied them to foreigners ('The franchise for foreigners, including local voting rights, is rejected'[53]). The party stubbornly defended Article 20 of the constitution which reserves the right to vote to citizens. In 1990, for example, the party successfully challenged in the courts Social Democratic legislation from Hamburg which extended the suffrage to foreigners. If foreigners chose not to integrate and naturalize, then they chose, in the logic of the CDU, not to accept or appreciate the core values of the republic. This meant they presented a danger to the free democratic order and were susceptible to political extremism. Thus the CDU/CSU faction in the *Bundestag* gave the rationale behind its objection to local voting rights as follows:

If the franchise were granted, the participation of foreign national parties in elections could not be avoided. Whoever in recent months has pursued the excesses of foreign extremism in the Federal Republic – the catchwords Kurdish terrorism and the appearance of fanatical Turkish nationalists suffice – knows that the last thing we need is campaign battles between left-wing and right-wing extremist foreign parties in the Federal Republic.[54]

Kohl's government sought to deny other rights to foreigners. The new Aliens Law states: 'Foreigners, while entering or residing in federal territory, are not, according to the Basic Law, equal to Germans' (Section III). The section also reminds that Article 11 of the constitution guarantees freedom of movement to citizens only. Moreover, the new

53 'Union legt Konzept für eine langfristige Regelung vor,' *Uid* (January 21, 1982): 12; also see 37. *Bundesparteitag*, p. 473.
54 *CDU/CSU Fraktion im Deutschen Bundestag Pressedienst* (August 5, 1987).

law stipulates that the human rights of free development of the personality (Article 2) and the sanctity of the family (Article 6) apply only to legal aliens. It follows, then, that the government's decision regarding an alien's residence permit is prior to his or her constitutional rights. With this legal logic, the Christian Democrats strengthened in various ways the powers of the police to monitor, sequester, and deport aliens.

The new law thus creates two legal classes of persons: first-class citizens and second-class denizens. But this Nuremberg Law for the 1990s does not distinguish between the two classes or justify their unequal relationship on the basis of race, nationality, or religion. The distinction and justification rest on one's commitment (or lack thereof) to the liberal principles of the constitution – something one demonstrates by *freely* choosing to naturalize. Those who *freely* choose not to naturalize are not guests but rather enemies of the republic. In other words, living in the Federal Republic long enough to be eligible for citizenship without becoming a citizen is taken as a threat to the basic free democratic order. Such persons represent the classic 'state within a state' so commonly used to refer to Poles in the eighteenth and nineteenth centuries. But the difference today is that the latter state is liberal rather than nationalist, the former (allegedly) illiberal rather than irredentist.

REMAKING THE PAST AND PRESENT SELF

As with their predecessors, the new interpretation and practice of *Ausländerpolitik* served to improve the image Christian Democratic leaders wanted to have of themselves and their people. As intimated in the second chapter, there had always been something quirky about West German liberal democracy. Although enshrining the idea of free choice, liberal democracy had come to West Germans as an imposition. In reality, the Allies had chosen the institutions that govern the West Germans. In reality, a technocratic state had taught them what values to embrace. By the 1980s, in other words, the West Germans faced the same paradox of Rousseau's Émile, who admits he was forced (by his mentor) to be free. Ultimately, liberalism makes little sense if one is forced to be liberal.

Christian Democrats, who did, in fact, want to escape the suspicions inherited from Hitler and the Holocaust, needed free choice to prove the genuine commitment to liberalism they felt in their hearts. But they could not find it. Neither they nor their ancestors had chosen the liberal constitution or founded the liberal republic. And nowadays West Germans were simply born into the liberal democratic order. They had no choice.

The new *Ausländerpolitik* enabled conservative leaders to fabricate free choice as if with a magic wand. Emphasizing migrants' right and need freely to choose or refuse citizenship made it appear as though West Germans freely choose it. It is difficult to read Christian Democratic position papers on naturalization without getting the impression that West Germans each and every day deliberately (or freely) re-commit themselves to the values embodied in the Basic Law. This is why it is so important that migrants make a choice. For their would-be fellow citizens regularly do the same thing. Moreover, Christian Democrats knew perfectly well that most aliens do not naturalize. The former wanted to make it appear that the latter freely choose to adhere to their premodern, illiberal traditions and eschew the modern liberal values associated with West German citizenship. For this makes the fact that West Germans remain modern and liberal seem like a deliberate (or free) choice. After all, they too could revive their old ways. They choose not to. In other words, by appearing to give migrants the freedom to reject liberalism, Christian Democrats were giving themselves the freedom they needed to be able comfortably to espouse it.

5

UNITED GERMANY: *BUNDESREPUBLIK* OR *DEUTSCHLAND*?

The population of the former GDR initially oriented itself mainly around the living standards of the old Federal Republic ... and not very much around the democratic values. The development of a democratic value system will demand considerable time. These developments thoroughly correspond to the experiences in the old Federal Republic following the war.

(From a study commissioned by the Federal Ministries for Technology and Research and for Labor and Social Order)[1]

INTRODUCTION

Before 1989, Germans used the term '*Wende*' to refer to the transition from the Schmidt to the Kohl government in 1982. This meaning vanished overnight between November 9 and 10, 1989. The real *Wende* became the revolution on the other side of the Berlin Wall and the subsequent Unification of the two Germanys. Doubtless this shift in meaning was justified. By October 1990, Germany had experienced far more than a change in political leadership. It now had new expanded

---

1 Hiltrud Nassmacher, 'Transformationsprozesse aus regionaler und lokaler Perspektive,' in Hiltrud Nassmacher, Oskar Niedermayer, and Hellmut Wollman, eds, *Politische Strukturen im Umbruch* (Berlin: Akademie Verlag, 1994), p. 1.

borders, 17 million new citizens, and a mountain of challenges to overcome.

Among the myriad problems confronting Germany, migration was paramount. Indeed, migration (or the desire for it) inspired the revolution and determined the collapse of the East German regime. Once the Krenz government opened the Wall and let its people vote with their feet, it had no real chance of surviving. Soon thereafter, migration (now mainly the threat of it in West German eyes) also set the pace and terms of Unification. For had Kohl not quickly promised reunification, he would have likely faced massive emigration from East Germans. Indeed, the exodus reached 2,000 per day by early 1990.

Migration thus forged united Germany. And although not all of the German Democratic Republic's people physically migrated west, all 17 million did on October 3, 1990 become newcomers (one might say stationary migrants) to the Federal Republic through Unification.[2] Add to this the 5.3 million resident aliens Germany registered at the end of 1990, not to mention the stream of refugees from East Europe after the lifting of the Iron Curtain (for example, nearly 500,000 in 1992, alone),[3] and it becomes clear that well over one quarter of united Germany's residents were migrants or newcomers of one sort or the other. There could be no more denying that Germany was an *Einwanderungsland*.

With the potential for mass emigration from inside and outside Germany on the horizon, anxiety soon surfaced that Germany would revive and revert to aggressive and atavistic nationalism in response to the problem. Literally hundreds of books, articles, and conferences addressed this theme.[4] Highly publicized attacks on foreigners' residences

2 Though the Preamble to the Basic Law did, from its inception, consider East Germans *de jure* citizens of the Federal Republic.

3 *The Week in Germany* (January 13, 1995): 2.

4 See, for instance, Peter Glotz, *Die deutsche Rechte* (Munich: Wilhelm Heyne, 1992); Klaus Farin and Eberhard Seidel-Pielen, *Rechtsruck* (Berlin: Rotbuch, 1992).

in Hoyerswerda in 1991, Rostock in 1992, and Solingen in 1993 (in which five Turks died) led fears of resurgent nationalism to burgeon. And in fact, both the number and intensity of criminal acts hostile to foreigners increased after Unification (2,426 in 1991 to 6,336 in 1992).[5] According to the Agency for the Protection of the Constitution, the number of right-wing extremist groups rose from 76 in 1991 to 82 in 1992, encompassing an estimated 41,900 members.[6] One survey found that three-quarters of polled Germans viewed the 'foreigner problem' as the most important issue in Germany.[7] Another reported that 64.9 per cent of polled Turks labeled xenophobia their greatest worry.[8] In response to growing xenophobia, the *Bundestag* in 1993 amended the constitution to toughen its Article 16 regarding political asylum. Germany again seemed a place neither comfortable nor safe for non-Germans.

But after the dust from Unification settled, these fears turned out to be unfounded. Although signs of resurgent nationalism remained visible in united Germany, the great plague of Germany's past failed to spread into much actual legislation hostile to foreigners, particularly those living in the Federal Republic. On the contrary, much legislation beneficial to foreigners was passed and proposed. At the same time, though, even more legislation hostile to (some) Germans both inside and outside the Federal Republic followed in the wake of Unification. Put differently, if Germany needed a systematic policy of inclusion and exclusion to deal with its migrant problem, an unabashedly nationalist strategy did not win the day.

Instead, a liberal strategy, with a zeal unmatched even by

5 Thomas Ohlemacher, 'Public Opinion and Violence Against Foreigners in the Reunified Germany,' *Zeitschrift für Soziologie* 23 (June 1994): 227.

6 *New York Times*, (October 21, 1993).

7 Claus Leggewie, *Druck von rechts* (Munich: Beck, 1993), p. 165.

8 Reported in Beauftragte der Bundesregierung für die Belange der Ausländer, *Bericht über die Lage der Ausländer in der Bundesrepublik Deutschland* 1993 (Bonn: Beauftragte der Bundesregierung für die Belange der Ausländer, 1994), p. 77.

the Allies after the war, won out. The new Germany did in fact bring more of the German nation together under one political roof, but the leaders of the expanded country took decisive action to prevent euphoric nationalism from changing significantly the republic's character. The republic was to be larger but in no fundamental way different from the smaller version of 1949–1990. And this meant the 17 million German newcomers from the east would have to be integrated just like the non-German newcomers from Europe's southern periphery.

EUPHORIC NATIONALISM AND RESURGENT RACISM

'What belongs together grows together.' These volkish-sounding words uttered shortly after the fall of the Wall by Willy Brandt – a man who fought much of his life against nationalism – revealed the nearly irresistible appeal of German nationalism in November 1989. A nation forcibly divided for four decades could again come together. And most Germans felt, like Brandt, that it was only natural that Germans unite. The West Germans were as willing to welcome their eastern brethren as the East Germans were eager to visit the West. As the latter first crossed over, they were met with much pageantry and 100 crisp D marks. The generosity persisted and intensified. The roughly 2.5 million Germans east of the Federal Republic who decided to move there received extensive and expensive public assistance to help them resettle (over DM10 billion in 1992).[9] Moreover, they gained immediate and automatic citizenship as stipulated in Article 116 of the Basic Law. The Germans who stayed in East Germany were offered an extraordinarily favorable exchange rate for their East German marks in July 1990. Later on October 3, the day of Unification, they became *de facto* citizens of the Federal Republic rather than

9 *Frankfurter Allgemeine Zeitung* (October 29, 1992): 3.

the mere *de jure* citizens they had been since 1949. In addition, the Kohl administration announced after the general elections of 1990 that it would allocate DM100 billion (over a tenth of the federal budget) for reconstruction and improvements in the eastern provinces (actually, DM113 billion was ultimately spent[10]).

Foreigners watched these developments with deep frustration. Integration had commenced in the 1970s but had progressed slowly. Foreigners (55 per cent of whom had lived in the Federal Republic for more than ten years, over 1 million of whom were born there, and all of whom combined paid roughly DM90 billion annually in taxes) had been told time and again by Bonn that it would take a long time before they would 'catch up' socio-economically with the West Germans. But the Chancellor promised East Germans, before any of them paid a single tax, that he would bring West German socio-economic standards to them in five short years. Although foreigners received some purely consultative political representation in various 'Foreigners' Councils,' the West German government had still not granted them even municipal voting rights. As seen above, years of restrictive requirements for naturalization left West Germany with the lowest rate of naturalization in the industrial world. Yet, according to Article 116 of the Basic Law, the estimated 8 million Germans living in the former Soviet bloc enjoyed a right to immediate German citizenship. And if that were not kick in the face enough, Germany picked up the tabs for the resettlers' transportation costs.

Put differently, the legislation aimed at Germans from the east was blatantly discriminatory and racist. As noted in the introduction, Article 116 granted citizenship on the basis of lineage rather than territory. The right of citizenship belonged to 'everyone . . . who, as a refugee or expellee of

10 Irwin Collier, 'German Economic Integration: The Case for Optimism,' in *From Bundesrepublik to Deutschland*, eds Michael Huelshoff, Andrei Markovits, and Simon Reich (Ann Arbor: The University of Michigan Press, 1993), p. 107.

German ethnicity, or as a spouse or descendant of such persons, has been admitted to the territory of the German Reich as it existed on December 31, 1937.'[11] In 1937, German ethnicity was defined by the racist Nuremberg Laws of 1935. Article 116 and the practices it sanctioned also helped to fuel the increasing hostility toward foreigners after Unification. As Germans began to realize that the costs of Unification would far exceed the optimistic projections of Chancellor Kohl in 1990, many began entertaining ideas of targeting foreigners as the ones who should bear the greatest hardships. Germans for whom Unification turned sour (particularly youths in the east) looked to foreigners as scapegoats and began verbally to demand and even physically to ensure their elimination from the land. Although neither the government nor the constitution ever sanctioned the maltreatment of foreigners, both sanctioned preferential treatment of Germans. Had the government further pursued or strengthened this policy, a systematic policy of discrimination based on nation would have developed. But it did not.

REVIVED LIBERALISM

Opposition and limitations to nationalism soon sprang up from various quarters. Esteemed President Richard von Weizsäcker led the way by frequently condemning xenophobic acts and attitudes. In the summer of 1991, Liselotte Funcke resigned as Commissioner for Aliens in bitter and public protest over the unfair treatment of foreigners. Kohl himself called the riots in Rostock 'a national disgrace.' Hundreds of other prominent personalities publicly condemned xenophobia and praised the idea of a 'multicultural society.'[12] Average German citizens organized demonstrations for foreigners far larger in numbers than those against

11 Quoted in William Rogers Brubaker, *Citizenship and Nationhood in France and Germany* (Cambridge, Mass.: Harvard University Press, 1992), p. 169.
12 See, for example, *Das Manifest der 60* (Munich: Beck, 1994).

them (such as the mass candlelight marches staged against racist violence).

Practical considerations also discredited a nationalist approach. At the time of Unification, 70 per cent of resident aliens in Germany possessed the irrevocable residence entitlement.[13] Poorly trained east German workers could hardly be expected productively to replace foreigners who had been on the job for years. Countless studies reported rates of productivity among east German workers far below rates in counterpart industries in the west (on average 50 per cent).[14] In diplomacy, Bonn's international restraints on anti-foreigner measures did not disappear. All members of the European Union continued to enjoy the unrestricted right to reside and work in Germany. The Treaty of Maastricht actually improved those rights by providing local voting rights to all European Union aliens (about 1.5 million) in Germany. Furthermore, the European Council took steps in 1993 to make dual citizenship easier (and therefore migrant naturalization likelier) in member states.[15] The Union's Treaty of Association with Turkey remained valid, and other such treaties with aspiring member states much closer to Germany in East Europe loomed. In 1991, Germany signed a Friendship Treaty with neighboring Poland which, by scrapping visa requirements for Polish visitors, made it much easier for Poles to work surreptitiously in Germany. The same treaty made provision for a limited number of temporary work permits to be distributed to Poles each year.

The most openly hostile legislation pertaining to foreigners came in July 1993 with the revision of the law

13 See H. Heyden, 'South–North Migration,' *International Migration* 29 (1991): 281–290.
14 A summary of the studies can be found in Gert Leptin, 'Systemvergleich: Wirtschaftssystem,' in *Handbuch zur deutschen Einheit*, eds Werner Weidenfeld and Karl-Rudolf Korte (Frankfurt: Campus, 1993), pp. 621–629.
15 Council of Europe, 'Second Protocol Amending the Convention on Reduction of Cases of Multiple Nationality,' *European Treaty Series*, No. 149 (Strasbourg: Council of Europe, 1993).

governing political asylum. However, the revision adversely affected only refugees residing outside Germany. Under the revised law, Germany began automatically rejecting applicants for political asylum who came from countries complying with the Geneva Convention for Refugees and the European Rights Convention. In addition, the government maintained the same policy for all countries which it deemed politically 'safe'; and all nine of Germany's contiguous neighbors earned the distinction. Practically, this meant that all applicants who entered Germany after July 1993 via land routes would automatically be turned away. Moreover, all applicants in foreign countries had to apply at the German embassy in their country and await a decision there. The policy was clearly designed to stop refugees before they reached the border, since at the time the law was amended, the Interior Ministry was rejecting 95 per cent of applications processed. The law worked. Whereas 1992 saw 440,000 applications, 1994 saw 127,000. The ministry also detected fewer illegal entries on Germany's eastern border in 1994 (11,321 compared to 29,834 in 1993).[16]

But the revised law was not nearly as tough on the roughly 1 million applicants already in Germany in 1993. Their basic welfare had to be guaranteed until their applications were completed – a process which often took years. And even once completed, further stays and appeals were not impossible. For instance, during the winter of 1994/95, the Ministry of the Interior placed a three-month moratorium on the expulsion of rejected Kurdish refugees and established a bilateral commission with Ankara to monitor the treatment of Kurdish returnees.[17] Of course, the new law affected in no way the over 5 million resident aliens.

At the same time, regulations regarding Germans living outside the republic tightened. For instance, after July 1991, ethnic Germans were required to apply for visas to Germany

16 *Deutschland Nachrichten* (June 23, 1995).
17 *The Week in Germany* (March 17, 1995).

in their homelands rather than simply show up at the border claiming the rights of Article 116. The Supreme Administrative Court ruled shortly thereafter that ethnic Germans living in lands that guarantee the rights of German minorities (for instance, Poland) should not expect to receive automatic asylum or citizenship based on Article 116. In 1992, the Kohl administration established an annual limit of 220,000 ethnic Germans permitted to naturalize. Social services available to them were also reduced to six months of language training and no more than fifteen months of social welfare payments. These new measures discouraged German immigration; the rate in 1994 was 56 per cent of the figure for 1992 and 90 per cent for 1993.[18]

As for new legislation aimed at foreigners in Germany, things improved. The new Aliens Law of 1991, as discussed in the previous chapter, significantly liberalized the requirements for citizenship. Moreover, in the wake of the fatal arson attack on a refugee dormitory in Solingen in 1993, the Kohl administration came under heavy political pressure from prominent members of its own government (the President of the Republic, the President of the *Bundestag*, and the Commissioner for Aliens to name a few), its coalition partner, and the opposition further to liberalize the requirements by permitting dual citizenship. The Kohl administration responded in 1994 with a proposal to grant automatic German citizenship to children under 18 whose parents had lived in Germany for at least ten years and one of whose parents had been born in the Federal Republic. The youngsters were allowed to possess the citizenship of Germany and their parents' country until they turned 18, at which time they had to choose to relinquish one.

Efforts to curb xenophobia sprang up. Between 1989 and 1995, state and federal governments banned ten neo-Nazi organizations,[19] and in 1995, a state court in Karlsruhe

18 *The Week in Germany* (November 25, 1994).
19 *The Week in Germany* (March 3, 1995).

sentenced Günter Deckert, the leader of the far right-wing National Democratic Party of Germany, to two years' imprisonment for inciting fear. A year earlier, the Federal Constitutional Court had ruled that denial of the Holocaust was not protected under freedom of expression. A year before that, parliament amended the Victims Indemnity Law to make foreign victims equal to Germans for benefits. In 1994, Kohl's government successfully proposed that the *Bundestag* expand the powers of the police and intelligence service to apprehend even more right-wing extremists, as well as to ban neo-Nazi symbols from public. This came two years after his government had earmarked DM20 million per year to counter violence against foreigners in the new eastern provinces. States and municipalities launched similar programs.[20] The measures proved effective. From 1993 to 1994, the number of reported hostile acts toward foreigners halved.[21]

INTEGRATION

No group, save the convicted neo-Nazis, experienced the minimal national solidarity in Germany more than the east German newcomers. What was originally celebrated as the coming together of a divided people soon became experienced as a takeover by foreign invaders. Words like 'invasion' (*'Einmarsch'*) and 'colonization' (*'Kolonisierung'*) swiftly appeared as common characterizations of Unification. Like foreigners, east Germans lived below the west German standard of living after Unification (for example, 70 per cent of the average west German household income[22] and 27 per cent of the average household's total assets[23]).

20 See, for instance, Reinhard Koch, 'Deeskalation von Jugendgewalt. Praktische Erfahrungen aus Sachsen-Anhalt,' *Aus Politik und Zeitgeschichte* (November 12, 1993): 16–23.

21 *Migration News Sheet* (March 1995).

22 For a thorough comparison of west vs. east German living standards, see Klaus Asche, 'Zur wirtschaftlichen Lage in den östlichen Bundesländern,' *Deutschland Archiv* (March 1994): 232–237.

23 *The Week in Germany* (February 17, 1995).

Furthermore, they soon heard from officials that the inequality would persist for at least a generation rather than five years. Like foreigners, east Germans suffered higher rates of unemployment than west Germans (13.5 per cent and 8.2 per cent respectively in 1994[24]). And as foreigners did throughout the 1970s and 1980s, east Germans started to organize among themselves to protest their situation. Nearly 20 per cent of them voted for the successor party to East Germany's Communist Party (PDS) in the federal elections in October 1994.

These similarities went beyond mere appearance. They stemmed from the fact that east Germans became objects of a liberal technocratic campaign of integration similar, if not identical, to the one devised for foreigners, which itself, as we have seen, took much from the one originally devised for West Germans after the war. And as with the latter groups, the logic of technocratic liberalism demanded the political subordination of east Germans. The politically subordinate position of foreigners was always obvious: as aliens, they never enjoyed full rights of political participaiton. The subordination of east Germans was more complicated because they became citizens at the time of Unification. However, Unification ultimately panned out as a systematic subjugation of east Germans. In the first place, west German political parties and personalities dominated the first free election in East Germany in March 1990 (spending a total of DM40 million). The CDU alliance and SPD captured over 70 per cent of the vote compared to 2.9 per cent for New Forum and Democracy Now and 16.3 per cent for the PDS. Referring to the influence of the West German parties, former East Berlin Mayor Pfarrer Albertz remarked: 'An invasion would have been more honest.'[25] What the Allies achieved during occupation through selective licensing, the West Germans achieved during Unification through money and

24 *The Week in Germany* (January 13, 1995).
25 Quoted in Michael Schneider, *Die abgetriebene Revolution* (Berlin: Elefanten Press, 1990), pp. 94–122.

marketing. Either way, the dependable liberal democratic parties triumphed.

Dominating both regimes, Christian Democrats were positioned to structure Unification as they wanted. The choice to annex the eastern provinces, as allowed in Article 23 of the Basic Law, meant not only that no new constitution would be drafted, but also that the conditions of Unification would not have to be ratified in a national plebiscite, just as the Basic Law was never ratified in 1949. Moreover, the east Germans were integrated into a federal structure in which they represented a minority *vis-à-vis* west Germans in both the *Bundestag* and *Bundesrat*. Hardly surprising, then, that a survey taken in Berlin in December 1990 found that 42.4 per cent of polled east Germans felt shut out of the Unification negotiations, while another 36.7 per cent felt they were merely onlookers.[26]

The Treaty of Unification gave sweeping power to Bonn. The overwhelming majority of East German laws and procedures went out of effect on October 3, 1990. Courts and police offices had to enforce new laws. Welfare agencies had to provide different services. Schools and universities had to adopt new curricula. Most notably, Chapter 6, Article 25 placed under the auspices of the Finance Ministry the Trust Agency (*Treuhandanstalt*), which controlled all East German industry. The entire civil service stood before reform designed to make it emulate the West German public sector (Chapter 5, Article 20). Furthermore, the Treaty stipulated that east German public servants could be dismissed if they were deemed incompetent, or were no longer needed, or had violated internationally recognized principles of humanity, or had worked for the Ministry of State Security or Office of National Security.[27] For the most part, west German officials

26 Jürgen Hoffmann, 'Abgesprungen, aber (noch) nicht angekommen,' *Berliner Linke* (June 3–9, 1991): 10.
27 See Gregg O. Kvistad, 'Accommodation or "Cleansing": Germany's State Employees from the Old Regime,' *West European Politics* 17/4(October 1994): 52–73.

thus acquired broad discretion over the destiny of countless East Germans not wholly unlike that given to the Allies in JCS 1067 or West German police in the Aliens Law of 1965.

Nor did the west Germans demur in exercising their power. They swiftly set about retraining, replacing, or terminating personnel. In the public sector, officials endeavored to purge so-called 'politicized incompetence'[28] left over from communist days. This often entailed replacing east with west Germans or seeking influential assistance from the latter. By late 1992, for instance, roughly 1,400 western federal and 8,400 western state administrators were working in leadership positions in the east.[29] In Brandenburg, for example, 52 per cent of high-level civil servants by 1993 were west Germans: 73 per cent in the Chancellory, 72 per cent in the Ministry of Justice, and 67 per cent in the Ministry of Finance. In addition, each of the eastern provinces took on west German 'partner provinces,' which regularly sent public servants on a temporary basis to the east to provide aid and assistance. During 1993, for instance, North Rhine-Westphalia sent 22 per cent (956) of its top civil servants to help in Brandenburg.[30] On the inverse side, an estimated 200,000 east Germans had left their public-service jobs by October 1992.[31]

The education system underwent similar changes. The Science Council and the Commissions on High School Structure in each province, all of which became dominated by west Germans, were charged with remaking the system of higher education and scientific research in east Germany

28 Hans-Ulrich Derlien, 'Intregration der Staatsfunktionäre in das Berufs-beamtentum: Professionalisierung und Säuberung,' in *Verwaltungs-reform und Verwaltungspolitik im Prozess der deutschen Einigung*, eds Wolfgang Seibel, Arthur Benz, and Heinrich Mäding (Baden-Baden: Nomos, 1993), p. 193.
29 Klaus Goetz, 'Rebuilding Public Administration in the New German Länder,' *West European Politics* (October 1993): 454.
30 Siegfried Grundmann, 'Zur Akzeptanz und Integration von Beamten aus den alten in den neuen Bundesländern,' *Deutschland Archiv* (January 1994): 31–42.
31 Goetz, 'Rebuilding Public Administration,' p. 461.

after the image of west Germany. With the powers granted them by Article 38 of the Treaty of Unification, the two bodies launched extensive reforms in curricula and personnel. Entire disciplines in the humanities and social sciences deemed 'close to the [communist] regime' ('regimenah') were either eliminated or fully restructured. In these disciplines, one study from 1994 concluded: 'There are hardly any professors from the east left.' The other disciplines experienced major personnel, if not curricular changes. The same study estimated that in the uncontaminated disciplines, west Germans eventually assumed about one-third of the academic positions.[32] In addition, the number of positions available in the many non-teaching research institutes of east Germany dropped from 31,000 in 1991 to 13,500 in 1994.[33] Similar drastic changes transpired in the secondary and primary schools as well as the public cultural and athletic institutions.[34] Taken together, these figures suggest a 'decommification' of the education system more extensive than was denazification. Neither, however, compares with the longstanding 'Berufsverbot' (hiring ban) against resident aliens in upper echelons (Beamtenshicht) of the civil service.

East Germans also had to be integrated into the west German labor market after October 3, 1990. Although the campaign often entailed the full-scale absorption of east German organizations and enterprises into their west German counterparts (for instance, in the case of the media[35] or organized labor[36]), its most significant feature wound up being the systematic deindustrialization of the eastern

32 Wolfgang Schluchter, 'Die Hochschulen in Ostdeutschland vor und nach der Einigung,' Aus Politik und Zeitgeschichte (June 24, 1994): 12–22.
33 Gerhard Neuweiler, 'Das gesamtdeutsche Haus für Forschung und Lehre,' Aus Politik und Zeitgeschichte (June 24, 1994): 3–11.
34 For documentation of these changes see the three volumes of Weissbuch: Unfrieden in Deutschland (Berlin: Kolog Verlag, 1992, 1993, 1994).
35 See Richard L. Merritt, 'Normalizing the East German Media,' Political Communication 11(1994): 49–66.
36 On this process, see Detlef Perner, 'Gewerkschaften,' in Weidenfeld and Korte, Handbuch zur deutschen Einheit, pp. 233–234.

provinces. Between 1989 and 1991 the GDP, in what some termed Germany's *Mezzogiorno*,[37] declined 40 per cent, industrial production 70 per cent, employment 40 per cent (a faster drop than in the United States after the Crash of 1929). While east Germans comprised over 20 per cent of Germany's population, east German GDP in 1994 constituted only 7.9 per cent of the total GDP, 2 per cent of total exports.[38] As the Trust Agency privatized its roughly 13,000 firms, the new owners (almost always west German firms) typically 'downsized' the personnel.[39] By 1993, more than half of the jobs which existed in 1989 in East Germany had disappeared.[40] By 1992, only 31 per cent of east Germans had continued working uninterruptedly in the same position they held before Unification. In 1989, 9.5 million people were employed in East Germany; in 1994, 6 million. In 1994 13.5 per cent of eligible workers were officially unemployed; yet another 20 per cent worked in the various 'job-creation' positions slotted for eventual termination. By 1994, over 1 million east Germans had fled west and about 500,000 were commuting back and forth.[41]

Put differently, west Germans wound up possessing and wielding far more power in East Germany than most east Germans originally expected. In September 1990, roughly 7 per cent of polled east Germans opposed the importation of west German elites; by November 1992, the figure had risen to 34 per cent. Indeed, west Germans residing in the east tied with Turks in the survey for the least-liked

37 John Hall and Udo Ludwig, 'Creating Germany's *Mezzogiorno?*,' *Challenge* (July–August 1993): 38–41.
38 Rudolf Hickel and Jan Priewe, *Nach dem Fehlstart* (Frankfurt: S. Fischer, 1994), p. 21.
39 For a thorough account of the Trust Agency's practices, see Siegbert Preuss, 'Die Treuhandanstalt,' *Fhw forschung* (April 22, 1993): 87–135.
40 Friederike Maier, 'Frauenerwerbstätigkeit in der vereinigten Bundesrepublik,' *Fhw forschung* (April 22, 1993): 23.
41 Horst Berger and Annett Schultz, 'Veränderung der Erwerbssituation in ostdeutschen Privathaushalten und Befindlichkeit der Menschen,' *Aus Politik und Zeitgeschichte* (April 22, 1994): 3–15.

newcomers in the eastern provinces.[42] In 1991, 49 per cent of questioned east Germans felt that most of their compatriots viewed Unification as a mistake.[43] In 1995, 16 per cent of polled east Germans (in contrast to 47 per cent of polled west Germans) said they were satisfied with Germany's corpus of laws,[44] while 53 per cent claimed Unification had turned out 'worse than I had expected' (43 per cent among west Germans).[45] Perhaps the east Germans did not qualify as the *Neger Europas*, but many (72 per cent according to one poll) started referring to themselves as 'second-class citizens' (*'Bürger zweiter Klasse'*).[46]

LIBERAL AND ILLIBERAL CITIZENS

East Germans received political treatment analogous to that prescribed for West Germans after the war and foreigners after the early 1970s because they were diagnosed with the same virus: namely, illiberalism. East Germans' political culture predictably came under close scrutiny after Unification; and the examiners did not like what they saw, for it was essentially the same pathological reaction to modernity and democracy they knew all too well.

East Germans, of course, grew up in an authoritarian society. Kurt Sontheimer, for instance, pointed out that the old prewar authoritarian political culture survived in the east despite the transformation to communism: 'This official political culture sanctioned by the Party and State thus built off German traditions ... of the leading Party and of the State with a decided priority over the needs and tendencies of the individual.' Furthermore, this political culture was 'tainted more strongly than that of the Federal Republic with

42 Grundmann, 'Zur Akzeptanz und Integration,' pp. 36–37.
43 *Der Spiegel* (July 22, 1991).
44 Reported in *The Week in Germany* (April 7, 1995).
45 *Der Spiegel* (3 July, 1995).
46 Ibid. Incidentally, only 22 per cent of West Germans viewed East Germans as 'second-class citizens.'

traditional attitudes which came out of German history. Thus the GDR society appeared in the judgement of some observers "more German" than the quickly modernizing and Americanizing Federal Republic.'[47] Dieter Frey outlined the characteristics individual east Germans learned to internalize under authoritarianism:

Most people in such systems suffer a chronic loss of control and helplessness. ... The *motivational deficits* are apathy, obesity, conformity to the existing norms, as well as low readiness for private initiative and self-responsibility. ... To the *affective-emotional* deficits belong chronic anxieties, strong future pessimism, low self-esteem, depression, low frustration tolerance, hopelessness and emotional instability. The consequences of these affective-emotional deficits are, among others, high suicide rates, high divorce rates, a high degree of alcoholism, drug abuse and a strong degree of disturbance in private relationships.[48]

If communism had not damaged them enough, east Germans faced rapid, disorienting change to boot. 'There exists a significant discrepancy,' concluded a study commissioned by the Federal Agency for All-German Efforts, 'between the behavioral repertoire of the erstwhile GDR citizens and the new challenges. The mental demands which pluralistic democracy and social market economy place on social actors are totally different.'[49] Another study implored

---

47 Kurt Sontheimer, *Grundzüge des politischen Systems der neuen Bundesrepublik Deutschland* (Munich: Piper, 1993), pp. 171–172; or see for the exact same argument Walter Gagel, 'Geschichte der politischen Bildung in der alten Bundesrepublik bis 1989,' in Adolf Noll and Lutz Reuter, eds, *Politische Bildung im vereinten Deutschland* (Opladen: Leske & Budrich, 1993), p. 13.

48 Dieter Frey, 'The Unification of Germany from the Standpoint of a Social Psychologist,' in *United Germany and the New Europe*, ed. Heinz Kurz (Brookfield: Edward Elgar, 1993), p. 60.

49 Katharina Belwe, *Befindlichkeit der Menschen in den neuen Bundesländern im ersten Jahr der deutschen Einheit (Teil II)* (Bonn: Gesamtdeutsches Institut, 1991), p. 3.

readers to keep in mind 'that 16 million GDR citizens have with the regime and system transformation lost their identity overnight.'[50] Moreover, 'the shock of the change of events runs deep, and for many east Germans the discontinuity of the political and societal history leads not only to a rift in their biography, but also in their individual identity.'[51] This 'cultural lag,'[52] this 'deep uprooting,'[53] this 'loss of control,'[54] this 'system transformation,'[55] this 'collapse of a holy, ordered world,'[56] revealed itself in the same kind of personal symptoms once diagnosed in prewar Germans and later in foreigners: 'anomie,' 'apathy,' 'aggression,' 'culture shock,' 'identity vacuum,' 'depression,' 'GDR nostalgia,' 'self-doubt,' 'suicide,' 'excessive consumption,' and 'criminality.'[57]

These personal problems spelled trouble for political behavior.

> The comprehensive feeling of malaise also encourages tendencies of political alienation which finds expression, for example, in a decreased interest in politics, a reduced willingness to participate in politics, a growing inclination toward political violence and a decrease in the acceptance of peaceful conflicts as the essential characteristic of democracy.[58]

50 Ulrich Becker, Horst Becker, and Walter Ruhland, *Zwischen Angst und Aufbruch* (Düsseldorf: ECON, 1992), p. 51.
51 Adolf Noll and Lutz Reuter, 'Einleitung,' in Noll and Reuter, *Politische Bildung*, p. 8.
52 Thomas Cusack and Wolf-Dieter Eberwein, 'The Endless Election: 1990 in the GDR,' in *Political Culture in Germany,* eds Dirk Berg-Schlosser and Ralf Rytlewski (New York: St Martin's, 1993), p. 209.
53 Gotthard Breit, 'Sozialstaat als Gegenstand des politischen Unterrichts am Beispiel Jugendarbeitslosigkeit und System der sozialen Sicherung,' in Noll and Reuter, *Politische Bildung*, p. 190.
54 Frey, 'The Unification of Germany,' p. 65.
55 Manuela Glaab and Karl-Rudolf Korte, 'Politische Kultur,' in Weidenfeld and Korte eds, *Handbuch zur deutschen Einheit*, p. 552.
56 Becker, Becker, and Ruhland, *Zwischen Angst und Aufbruch*, p. 124.
57 See the works cited in this paragraph, all of which use some of these labels.
58 Max Kasse, 'Innere Einheit,' in Weidenfeld and Korte, *Handbuch zur deutschen Einheit*, p. 378.

Thus, 'despite great emancipatory accomplishments during the collapse in October/November 1989, a political cultural continuity in values of the petit bourgeois and the authoritarian state traditions came to the fore: etatism, unpolitical subjectivity, aversion to conflict, formalism, need for security.'[59]

East Germans, in other words, had not yet experienced 'inner identification' with liberal democracy, had not yet made it their 'way of life' (to use concepts earlier applied to foreigners and West Germans respectively[60]).

Citizens of the former GDR have already developed affective ties to their new political community. However, these are not overflow consequences from satisfaction with politics and democracy or primarily politically motivated. On the contrary, they are either rooted in historical experience and social relations or closely linked to the economic benefits that are expected from belonging to this political community. With regard to this latter aspect these ties will be affected by any disappointment of economic hopes.[61]

Similarly, Kohl's success in the first free elections in East Germany was viewed by many, on the left naturally, as evidence of an opportunistic and gullible electorate susceptible to demagoguery and, therefore, unreliable for democracy.[62] Still others warned that even those east Germans who appeared to have made a quick conversion to Western norms and values were likely sporting a mere '*Pseudo-Identität.*'[63]

59 Manuela Glaab and Karl-Rudolf Korte, 'Politische Kultur,' in ibid., pp. 552–553.
60 See pp. 99 and 38 above.
61 Bettina Westle, 'Changing Aspects of National Identity,' in Berg-Schlosser and Rytlewski, *Political Culture*, p. 291. For a similar argument, see U. Feist, 'Zur politischen Akkulturation der vereinten Deutschen,' *Aus Politik und Zeitgeschichte*, Vol. 11–12 91 (1991): 21–32.
62 For example, K. Sieger, 'Opinion Research in East Germany – A Challenge to Professional Standards,' *International Journal of Public Opinion Research* 2/4(1990): 323–344.
63 Katharina Belwe, *Befindlichkeit (Teil II)*, p. 5.

'GDR nostalgia'[64] also worried west Germans. Many East Germans seemed to want to escape the present by romanticizing the way things were under communism. Polls which found a positive attitude toward the years 1933–1939 among nearly half of West Germans had alarmed elites four decades earlier.[65] In 1993, Bettina Westle reported that 50 per cent of east Germans were proud to have been citizens of the GDR. 'This,' she concluded, 'can be interpreted as a "new myth of the social welfare in the former GDR" and hints at a political instability in the eastern part of Germany, comparable to the one in the FRG in the 1960s.'[66] Of course, 'idealization of the homeland'[67] had since the 1970s been seen as a wellspring for extremists, like Islamic fundamentalists, among foreigners.

Accordingly, in the west emerged great concern over the potential for political extremism in the east. 'Vigilant democrats' had 17 million new suspects. Many analysts saw the rise in neo-Nazi activities and organizations in the east as part of a pathological response to abrupt, disorienting change: 'the reasons for the increase of the number of rightwing extremists seem to be ... the feeling of social discrimination, the lack of other traditionally established political orientations, the lack of experience in dealing with strangers and practical everyday problems.'[68]

Another study concluded:

> The sum total of all the frustrations becomes vented in slogans like 'Germany for the Germans – Foreigners Out!' Violent hooligans

64 See, for example, *Der Spiegel* (November 11, 1991).
65 See p. 22 above.
66 Bettina Westle, 'Changing Aspects,' p. 281.
67 Ursula Neumann, *Erziehung ausländischer Kinder* (Düsseldorf: Pädagogischer Verlag Schwann, 1980), p. 23.
68 Hans-Gerd Jaschke, 'Subcultural Aspects of Right-Wing Extremism,' in Berg-Schlosser and Rytlewski, *Political Culture*, p. 132. Also see Peter Ködderitzsch and Leo A. Müller, *Rechtsextremismus in der DDR* (Göttingen: Lamuv, 1990); or Kurt Hirsch and Peter B. Heim, *Von links nach rechts. Rechtsradikale Aktivitäten in den neuen Bundesländern* (Munich: Goldmann, 1991).

and applauding observers do not want to accept that indigent refugees, victims of political persecution, or religious minorities are being integrated into the commonwealth. Instead, the alleged uniform, homogeneous society is preferred.[69]

Others viewed persistent support for the PDS, 'where a large part of the left-wing extremist potential in the new federal states found its home,'[70] as evidence that the 'authoritarian-repressive structures of the society have not yet really been overcome.'[71]

But west German intellectuals knew how to combat the problem: re-education. It would no doubt take a 'massive information campaign'[72] to effect the change to a modern liberal outlook.[73] Pedagogues delineated the critical elements of 'a political education in the new federal states which aims successfully to build off the emancipatory traditions of Western modernity and which should contribute to the productive solution of the identity crises of the new federal citizens':

1 A confrontation free of taboos with the damaged identity of the individuals which formed principally under the political conditions of 'real socialist' society.

2 A broadening of the emancipatory potential (however deformed) of the GDR citizens that arose in the outward and inward tension with the political reality of the GDR and also in relation to possibilities for solving problems of social development which point beyond the GDR.

69 Glaab and Korte, 'Politische Kultur,' in Weidenfeld and Korte, *Handbuch zur deutschen Einheit,* p. 554.
70 Thomas Lillig, 'Extremismus,' in ibid., p. 280.
71 Hans-Joachim Maaz, 'Psychosoziale Aspekte im deutschen Einigungsprozess,' *Aus Politik und Zeitgeschichte* (May 3, 1991): 4.
72 Frey, 'The Unification of Germany,' p. 69.
73 See the prescriptions in Hans-J. Misselwitz, 'Politische Bildung in den neuen Ländern. In Verantwortung für die Demokratie in ganz Deutschland,' *Aus Politik und Zeitgeschichte* (September 16, 1991): 3–8; or Bernd Lüdkemeier and Michael Siegel, 'Zur Situation der politischen Bildung in den neuen Bundesländern,' *Aus Politik und Zeitgeschichte* (June 12, 1992): 32–38.

3 The establishment of intercultural learning processes between people from the west and east.[74]

'Confrontation with the damaged identity,' 'broadening of
the emancipatory potential,' 'intercultural learning processes' –these, or slight variations, were concepts common
to *Ausländerpädagogik* and to the Allied re-education campaign.

And, as with those campaigns, success was expected to
take a long time in the resocialization of east Germans. Karl
Rudolf-Korte and Manuela Glaab underscored that

the achievement of outer unity is not synonymous with
an inner unity: the chasm between the experience
horizons and life worlds of the Germans in east and
west mean that two political cultures grate against each
other. . . . Inner unity . . . develops only slowly.[75]

For, according to Hans-Joachim Maaz, 'democracy cannot
. . . be put on like a coat, rather it must take root in the minds
and hearts. . . . Democracy can only prevail . . . if it begins
in the souls of men.'[76] Katharina Belwe predicted that 'it will
take a longer individual and collective learning process
before the east German citizens can be made equal to the
citizens of the old federal states in competition for jobs but
also political and social positions.'[77] In the interim, concluded another study:

It is necessary for a lot of younger, still untrained
talents from the East to come to the West and learn as
quickly as possible the necessary know-how, and for
Western experts to go to the East for a certain time in
order to exemplify modern models of decision-making.

---

74 Wolfgang Dümcke, 'Politische Bildung und Identitätskrise,' in Noll
and Reuter, *Politische Bildung*, p. 48.
75 Rudolf Korte and Glaab, 'Politische Kultur,' in Weidenfeld and Korte,
Handbuch zur deutschen Einheit, p. 555.
76 Hans-Joachim Maaz, 'Psychosoziale Aspekte im deutschen Einigings-
prozess,' *Aus Politik und Zeitgeschichte* (May 3, 1991): 4.
77 Belwe, *Befindlichkeit*, p. 3.

These top positions should probably be filled by Western managers for a short time only, to decrease envy and the impression that the West will take all the important positions.[78]

The transitional phase, because of the demanding changes confronting east Germans, would likely witness some frustration with liberal democracy. But as Max Kasse reminded, 'it took the "old" Federal Republic from its inception in 1949 some twenty years to be accepted by its own citizens as a democracy.' 'The [political] identification of the citizens of the new states ... corresponds to the situation in West Germany in the 1950s and cannot be labeled a legitimacy cushion [*Legitimitätspolster*] for the regime.'[79]

CONCLUSION

Common perceptions notwithstanding, Unification demonstrated the Federal Republic's liberal credentials. West German leaders surrendered neither their positions nor their attitudes to nationalists. Nor did they, as good nationalists should, treat their east German brethren as equals. Rather, the latter became marked in their new polity, like the foreigners who came there before them, as citizens of lower rank. They were indeed called citizens (*Bürger*) but never without qualification. For foreigners, it was '*unsere ausländischen Mitbürger*'; for East Germans, either '*ex-DDR-Bürger*,' '*Bürger aus den neuen Bundesländern*,' or simply '*neue Bundesbürger*.' These qualifiers functioned as the scarlet letters of technocratic liberalism. They marked their bearers as illiberals and, therefore, untrustworthy citizens. Unlike the heroine of the famous story, however, east Germans and foreigners were not forever condemned. They could shed their letters as soon as they could convince their liberal mentors of their genuine, inner conversion to liberalism.

78 Frey, 'The Unification of Germany,' p. 70.
79 Kasse, 'Innere Einheit,' pp. 373, 376.

Technocratic liberalism brought much welcomed change to Germany following the war. It helped to transform a belligerent, loathsome society into a peaceful, admirable one. In retrospect, its approach of granting true political equality only gradually and cautiously seems appropriate as a response to Hitler's defeated Germany. But is it not time to question its continued need and desirability? Do foreigners and east Germans really constitute threats on a par with Hitler's Nazis?

BIBLIOGRAPHY

Abadan-Unat, Nermin (1976). *Turkish Workers in Europe*. Leiden: E. J. Brill.

Adorno, T.W., Frenkel-Brunswik, Else, Levinson, Daniel J., and Sanford, R. Nevitt (1950). *The Authoritarian Personality*. New York: Harper & Brothers.

Almond, Gabriel and Verba, Sidney (1963). *The Civic Culture*. Princeton: Princeton University Press.

Almond, Gabriel and Verba, Sidney (eds) (1980). *The Civic Culture Revisited*. Boston: Little, Brown & Company.

Ardagh, John (1987). *Germany and the Germans*. New York: Harper & Row.

Baker, Kendall, Dalton, Russell, and Hildebrandt, Kai (1981). *Germany Transformed*. Cambridge, Mass.: Harvard University Press.

Baldwin, Peter (ed.) (1990). *Reworking the Past: Hitler, the Holocaust, and the Historians' Debate*. Boston: Beacon Press.

Balfour, Michael (1982). *West Germany: A Contemporary History*. New York: St Martin's.

Balibar, Étienne and Wallerstein, Immanuel (1991). *Race, Nation, Class*. London: Verso.

Bark, Dennis L. and Gress, David R. (1989). *A History of West Germany*, vol. I. Oxford: Basil Blackwell.

Berg-Schlosser, Dirk and Rytlewski, Ralf (eds) (1993). *Political Culture in Germany*. New York: St Martin's.

Blackbourn, David and Eley, Geoff (1984). *The Peculiarities of German History*. Oxford: Oxford University Press.

Brickner, Richard (1943). *Is Germany Incurable?* Philadelphia: J.B. Lippincott Co.

Brubaker, William Rogers (ed.) (1989). *Immigration and the Politics of Citizenship in Europe and North America*. Lanham: University Press of America.

Brubaker, William Rogers (1992). *Citizenship and Nationhood in France and Germany.* Cambridge, Mass.: Harvard University Press.

Bullock, Alan (1952). *Hitler: A Study in Tyranny.* London: Odhams Press.

Butler, Rohan D'O. (1941). *The Roots of National Socialism 1783–1933*. London: Faber & Faber.

Castles, Stephen and Godula, Kosack (1985). *Immigrant Workers and Class Structure in Western Europe*. Oxford: Oxford University Press.

Childs, David (1981). *West Germany, Politics and Society.* New York: St Martin's Press.

Conradt, David (1989). *The German Polity.* New York: Longman.

Craig, Gordon (1982). *The Germans*. New York: Meridian.

Crick, Bernard (1992). *In Defence of Politics*. Chicago: University of Chicago Press.

Dahrendorf, Ralf (1967). *Society and Democracy in Germany.* New York: W.W. Norton.

Dornberg, John (1976). *The New Germans: Thirty Years After.* New York: Macmillan.

Edinger, Lewis Joachim (1986). *West German Politics*. New York: Columbia University Press.

Evans, Richard (1989). *In Hitler's Shadow.* New York: Pantheon.

Fain, Haskell (1970). *Between Philosophy and History.* Princeton: Princeton University Press.

Fromm, Erich (1941). *Escape from Freedom*. New York: Rinehart.

Gay, Peter (1968). *Weimar Culture*. New York: Harper & Row.

Grass, Günter (1990). *Two States – One Nation?* San Diego: Harcourt Brace Jovanovich.

Habermas, Jürgen (ed.) (1985). *Observations on 'The Spiritual Situation of the Age.'* Cambridge: MIT Press.

Hancock, M. Donald (1989). *West Germany: The Politics of Democratic Corporatism*. Chatham: Chatham House Publishers.

Herbert, Ulrich (1990). *A History of Foreign Labor in Germany, 1889–1980*. Ann Arbor: University of Michigan Press.

Huelshoff, Michael, Markovits, Andrei, and Reich, Simon (eds) (1993). *From Bundesrepublik to Deutschland*. Ann Arbor: The University of Michigan Press.

Inglehart, Ronald (1990). *Culture Shift in Advanced Industrial Society.* Princeton: Princeton University Press.

James, Harold and Stone, Marla (eds) (1992). *When the Wall Came Down*. London: Routledge.

Jaspers, Karl (1967). *The Future of Germany.* Chicago: University of Chicago Press.

Katzenstein, Peter (1987). *Policy and Politics in West Germany.* Philadelphia: Temple University Press.

Krane, R.E. (ed.) (1975). *Man Power Mobility Across Cultural Boundaries.* Leiden: E.J. Brill.

Krane, R.E. (ed.) (1979). *International Labor Migration in Europe.* New York: Praeger.

Kubat, D. (ed.) (1984). *Politics of Return.* New York: Center for Migration Studies.

Kurz, Heinz (ed.) (1993). *United Germany and the New Europe.* Brookfield: Edward Elgar.

Laski, Harold (1943). *Reflections on the Revolution of Our Time.* London: George Allen & Unwin.

Layton-Henry, Zig (ed.) (1990). *The Political Rights of Migrant Workers in Western Europe.* London: Sage.

Mayer, Arno J. (1981). *The Persistence of the Old Regime.* New York: Pantheon.

Meinecke, Friedrich (1950). *The German Catastrophe,* trans. Sidney Fay. Boston: Beacon.

Merkle, Peter (1963). *The Origins of the West German Republic.* New York: Oxford University Press.

Merkle, Peter (1989). *The Federal Republic of Germany at Forty.* New York: New York University Press.

Miller, Mark J. (1981). *Foreign Workers in Western Europe.* New York: Praeger.

Moore, Barrington (1966). *Social Origins of Dictatorship and Democracy.* Boston: Beacon.

Mosse, George (1966). *The Crisis of German Ideology.* London: Weidenfeld & Nicolson.

Mosse, George (1970). *Germans and Jews.* New York: Howard Fertig.

Parsons, Talcott (1949). *Essays in Sociological Theory.* Glencoe, Ill.: Free Press.

Popper, Karl (1945). *The Open Society and Its Enemies,* vol. II. London: Routledge.

Pronay, Nicholas and Wilson, Keith M. (eds) (1985). *The Political Re-Education of Germany and Her Allies after World War II.* Totowa: Barnes & Noble Books.

Ringer, Fritz (1969). *The Decline of the German Mandarins.* Cambridge, Mass.: Harvard University Press.

Rist, R.C. (1978). *Guestworkers in Germany: The Prospects for Pluralism.* New York: Praeger.

Robin, Ron (1995). *The Barbed-Wire College.* Princeton: Princeton University Press.

Rogers, Rosemarie (ed.) (1985). *Guests Come to Stay: the Effects of European Labor Migration on Sending and Receiving Countries.* Boulder, Col.: Westview Press.

Rosenberg, Arthur (1965). *A History of the German Republic*, trans. I.F.D. Morrow and L.M. Sieveking. New York: Russell & Russell.

Schaffner, Bertram (1948). *Fatherland: A Study of Authoritarianism in the German Family.* New York: Columbia University Press.

Shirer, William (1960). *The Rise and Fall of the Third Reich.* New York: Simon & Schuster.

Spragens, Thomas (1981). *The Irony of Liberal Reason.* Chicago: The University of Chicago Press.

Stern, Fritz (1961). *The Politics of Cultural Despair.* Berkeley: University of California Press.

Stern, Fritz (1992). *The Failure of Illiberalism: Essays on the Political Culture of Modern Germany.* New York: Columbia University Press.

Tent, James F. (1982). *Mission on the Rhine.* Chicago: University of Chicago Press.

Veblen, Thorsten (1915). *Imperial Germany and the Industrial Revolution.* London: Macmillan.

Vermeil, Edmond (ed.) (1955). *The Third Reich.* London: Weidenfeld & Nicolson.

Watson, Alan (1993). *The Germans: Who Are They Now?* Chicago: Edition Q.

Weber, Max (1949). *The Methodology of the Social Sciences*, eds Edward Shils and Henry Finch. Glencoe, Ill.: The Free Press.

Wilson, Woodrow (1893). *The State.* Boston: D.C. Heath.

INDEX